# You Are Everything

# Everything Is You

## Michele Doucette

You Are Everything: Everything Is You

Copyright © 2011 by Michele Doucette, St. Clair Publications

All rights reserved. No part of this publication may be reproduced or transmitted in any form or by any means, electronic or mechanical, including photocopying, recording, or by any information storage and retrieval system, without written permission from the author.

ISBN 978-1-935786-17-7

Printed in the United States of America by

St. Clair Publications

PO Box 726

McMinnville, TN   37111-0726

http://stan.stclair.net

One of the biggest challenges of spiritual evolution is the cultivation of humility. We need to have enough humility to enable us to recognize those who have genuinely reached a higher stage of development than our own, and then we need to have enough courage to aspire to *meet them* where they are. If a spiritual teacher is authentic, he or she will never finally be satisfied until the student either equals or surpasses the teacher's attainment. A true teacher is someone who doesn't want followers, but rather wants *authentic partners* in this great task of evolutionary transformation.

Andrew Cohen (EnlightenNext Magazine)

# Table of Contents

| | |
|---|---|
| Dedication | 1 |
| Special Message | 2 |
| Author's Note | 12 |
| Reviews | 13 |
| Cyclic Universe Theory | 21 |
| The Unified Field | 30 |
| Vedic Science of Consciousness | 43 |
| The Proof | 51 |
| The Power Lies Within | 63 |
| Mindfulness | 74 |
| Positive Living | 94 |
| Positive Energy Quotes | 109 |
| Life Force Energy | 115 |
| Notable Comparisons | 132 |
| Passion | 143 |
| Know Thyself | 145 |
| Additional Pertinent Messages | 153 |
| Conclusion | 161 |
| Bibliography | 168 |

Websites ............................................................................ 179
About the Author .............................................................. 198

# Dedication

It was in reflecting on the March 11, 2011 earthquake that devastated Japan, triggering a huge tsunami that slammed into the north eastern coast of the country, moving the coastline of this country by as much as 4 metres (13 feet) and thereby shifting the earth on its axis (perhaps by as much as 6.5 inches), that I sat down to begin this book.

It is for these planetary brothers and sisters that I dedicate this tome.

# Special Message

Highly radioactive water has been leaking directly into the sea from a damaged pit near a crippled reactor at the Fukushima Nuclear Power Station.

Dr. John Price, nuclear expert and former member of the Safety Policy Unit at the UK's National Nuclear Corporation, has warned that it could take 50 to 100 years before the nuclear fuel rods have cooled enough to be removed (meaning that radiation leaks will continue). The brave souls that have been battling the situation are expected to die from radiation sickness.

By definition, "a meltdown is the severe overheating of the core of a nuclear reactor that results in either the partial or full liquefaction of its uranium fuel and supporting metal lattice, at times with the atmospheric release of deadly radiation. Partial meltdowns usually strike a core's middle regions instead of the edge, where temperatures are typically lower."[1]

It becomes even more heartbreaking when it takes a crisis of this magnitude to prompt a reassessment of nuclear power around the world.

The truth is "that even in the best-case scenario, the environmental and human consequences of this disaster will be enormous. The potential impact of a worst-case scenario is beyond most people's comprehension. To give an indication of the amount of radioactive material involved, the total capacity of the three reactors that were operating at the time of the earthquake was *double* that of the Chernobyl number 4 reactor that exploded 25 years ago in the Ukraine. To this, you have to add the radioactivity in the spent fuel pools of all 6 units and of the shared spent fuel pool."[2]

---

[1] New York Times (April 12, 2011). *From Afar, A Vivid Picture of*

[2] Ibid.

Even if the radioactivity "does not travel far, the release of just a fraction would have incalculable consequences for human beings and the environment." [3]

In a CNN broadcast dated March 18, 2011, Dr. Michio Kaku, a world renowned CUNY theoretical physicist, pointed out that "Chernobyl involved one reactor and only 57.6 tons of the reactor core went into the atmosphere." [4]

By comparison, the Fukushima Daiichi disaster immediately involved six reactors, with the IAEA (International Atomic Energy Agency, a UN Agency) documenting a total of "2,800 tons of highly radioactive old reactor cores" [5] escaping into the atmosphere.

---

[3] Kyodo News (March 28, 2011). *Can there be a silver lining to Japan's nuclear crisis?* News article accessed on April 2, 2011 at http://english.kyodonews.jp/news/2011/03/81489.html
[4] Nichols, Bob. (May 29, 2011) *Fukushima: How Many Chernobyl's Is It?* news article accessed on May 30, 2011 at http://www.shoah.org.uk/2011/05/29/fukushima-how-many-chernobyls-is-it/
[5] Ibid.

As of April 13, 2011, with the threat level having been raised from five to seven, Japan has finally admitted that Fukushima is in the same league as Chernobyl.

The threat increase "was recorded on the international scale overseen by the International Atomic Energy Agency (IAEA) and reflects concerns about long-term health risks as radioactive material continues to be emitted into the air, soil and seawater." [6]

---

[6] Peterkin, Tom. (April 13, 2011) *Thirty-two days after disaster struck, Japan finally admits Fukushima is in same league as Chernobyl* news article located at
http://www.scotsman.com/news/Thirtytwo-days-after-disaster-struck.6750834.jp

In further comparative terms, "simple division tells us there are at least 48.6 Chernobyl's in the burning old reactor cores pumping fiery isotopes into the Earth's atmosphere. It is no stretch to say Fukushima Daiichi's six reactors, and the dry holding pools for old reactor cores, are equal to more than 50 Chernobyl disasters." [7]

As of April 20, 2011, new data from the Japanese National Police Agency has shown that two-thirds of the victims identified in the March 11 earthquake and tsunami were elderly, and almost all of them drowned.

Adding those who are still missing, the earthquake and resulting tsunami killed an estimated 27,500 people. The police agency stated that nearly 93 percent of the victims drowned. Others perished in fires, were crushed to death or died from other causes.

---

[7] Nichols, Bob. (May 29, 2011) *Fukushima: How Many Chernobyl's Is It?* news article accessed on May 30, 2011 at http://www.shoah.org.uk/2011/05/29/fukushima-how-many-chernobyls-is-it/

In a news release [8] dated May 18, 2011, officials from the Tokyo Electric Power Company (TEPC) have admitted that "fuel in Reactor 1 of the Fukushima Daiichi nuclear complex melted just 16 hours after the devastating earthquake and tsunami hit the area." [9]

Shortly after this announcement was made, *The Telegraph* reported that "two more Fukushima reactors may soon suffer a meltdown as well. Efforts to cool the fuel in Reactors 2 and 3 have failed, and experts say that if the reactors cores have not already melted, they soon will." [10]

As reported on June 9, 2011, with the Japanese government having admitted that Fukushima reactors have likely melted through, it may be that this worst case nuclear accident possibility is now a reality. [11]

---

[8] http://www.telegraph.co.uk/news/worldnews/asia/japan/8517861/Japan-meltdown-feared-at-two-more-Fukushima-reactors.html

[9] http://www.naturalnews.com/032437_Fukushima_nuclear_meltdown.html

[10] Ibid.

[11] http://www.naturalnews.com/032657_Fukushima_meltdown.html

Currently, all of the "Northern Hemisphere inhabitants [which also includes Japan] are suffering internal radioactive contamination from [the] Fukushima Daiichi reactors." [12]

It is also known that radioactive exposures "are cumulative for each human, animal and plant" [13] which means that the mutated genetic codes shall continue to be passed onto offspring in each of these different categories, which may end up spawning "a new assortment of radiation-degraded mutants" [14] in both human and other life forms.

Clearly, this is a situation that continues to worsen every day.

David Rainoshek, M.A., has written a special report entitled *We Are All Fukushima: An Integral Perspective on the Meanings and Promises of Disaster*.

---

[12] Nichols, Bob. (May 29, 2011) *Fukushima: How Many Chernobyl's Is It?* news article accessed on May 30, 2011 at http://www.shoah.org.uk/2011/05/29/fukushima-how-many-chernobyls-is-it/
[13] Ibid.
[14] Ibid.

Courtesy of this document, you will be presented with a series of perspectives on how humanity has arrived at such a disastrous position (which also includes why we, the collective, are all partially responsible), including what this enormous event means. [15]

For continually updated Fukushima news, articles and information, please take the time to visit Natural News. [16]

My heart weeps for the loss of life in Japan, total numbers still unknown. In situations such as these – when Mother Nature shakes us up, courtesy of powerful earthquakes and massive tsunami's; when there is not enough time to get to safety; when the struggle becomes more than mere survival, as is now the case – that I struggle to find the message.

Mother Earth, on the other hand, has been speaking ever so loudly.

---

[15] http://www.naturalnews.com/downloads/We-Are-All-Fukushima.pdf
[16] http://www.naturalnews.com/Fukushima.html

Having been raped and abused for thousands of years, she, too, weeps.

We have polluted the oceans and rivers (her womb) in the flushing of pharmaceuticals down the toilet; the deliberate dumping of harmful materials into her rivers, waterways and oceans; the use of chemicals and non-biodegradable detergents; oil pollution, and the discharge of untreated or under treated sewage.

We have polluted the air (her breath) through the burning of fossil fuels (which create acid rain) and deforestation (which creates carbon dioxide); the continued use of aerosol sprays; the discarding of leaking refrigeration and air conditioning equipment in community landfills, and driving energy deficient vehicles.

We have ravaged the earth (her body) through mining; blasting; the use of chemical fertilizers, pesticides and insecticides; the careless disposal of toxic substances (which also includes batteries), and the use of radioactive materials.

Is it any wonder that we are now feeling her wrath?

The time is now to change the way we think about others, and act toward others, including Mother Earth.

Clearly, there is no better time to become joy, love, peace, kindness, compassion, cooperation, wisdom, harmony, empathy, goodwill and strength.

## Author's Note

You are everything; everything is you. These words are so very powerful, and, yet, understood by so few.

Given that energy cannot be destroyed, we know that energy is forever changing form. In this way, you could say that the energy of the universe is constantly being recycled. So, too, do we change form (masculine or feminine) with each new rebirth (incarnation) on this earth plane. In truth, we are also changing form *during* each lifetime as well, meaning that as we expand in both love and wisdom, we become more enhanced versions of our original selves. This clearly means that we, too, are also being recycled from the same stuff.

Quantum physics states that substance comes into existence through actual observation, meaning that when a mind thinks something into existence, it becomes real. Thus, *energy is both conscious* (fully aware, deliberate and intentional) *and infinite* (boundless and endless).

The ancients were well aware of this truth, of this premise.

# Reviews

With her latest book, *You Are Everything: Everything Is You*, Michele continues to prove, beyond any doubt, that as her consciousness expands, so, too, does her work.

Herein, Michele touches, and expands upon, many aspects of spirituality, all of which will serve to benefit both the beginner as well as the advanced individual, both of whom are on their own individual journey (of enlightenment).

I wholeheartedly endorse this latest publication.

Elio Serra, USA

*You Are Everything: Everything Is You* is another truly excellent work. I simply do not know how you can piece all of this information together, using the many sources at your disposal. You have quite the gift at being able to remember the essence of various authors, on the subject matter at hand, before summing it all up in your own way. Speaking of myself, I am not such a detailed person. While I understand quickly, I understand only the whole, as it were. I do not see details as being overly important and sometimes this causes problems. All this to simply say that while I thoroughly enjoyed reading this newest work, I would not be able to explain, in any great detail, what it is that you have written. To sum it up, if I may, your writing has to be experienced to be enjoyed.

Jean-Guy Poirier, Canada

In reading Michele's streaming edition of the forces at work in the world, in *You Are Everything: Everything Is You*, while grasping for a positive perspective for the loss of life and danger to the healthy balance of life (from the effects of tsunami's, earthquakes and wars), one must breathe deeply while reading through the lengthy list of writers and theories to reach the heart of what Michele arrives at in the final chapters.

The understanding reached is well worth the struggle of following the short versions of so many erudite writers of new age understandings of the events unfolding in the world today.

I feel good about adding to Michele's text in that in the Indigenous mind, the events happening, and the destruction taking place, are the derisive characteristics of life.

These happen as a direct result of neglect of the sacred laws governing our relationship with the Creator and with Mother Earth.

If you read the descriptions of the universe as a torus, like a smoke ring ever falling back in on itself, the shapes and placement of the galaxies makes perfect sense.

The understanding is that the earth and life are in a constant state of derision, and with the male force ruling the direction of the planet, you end up with a doubly destructive energy in everyone's life.

Bringing the harmonious feminine force of the healing heart, and the maternal tender aspects of life, to the moment; some balance is achieved, yet only enough to slow down the destructive forces, which does not repair the continual damage currently being done worldwide.

Years ago, I saw my own version of these events and passed these teachings on (after clearly seeing the poison on the waters spreading throughout the oceans that will affect even the Atlantic and the St Lawrence). This is a form of madness and will cause a rise in aggressive behavior. Yet, in all of this, the Creator is just playing with us; it is our option to wake up to the truth of our own actions and beliefs.

We each are capable and responsible to live the positive explosion of life, creating healing waves to flood the universe with light and love, for the power in our own souls is of the same magnitude as the power in the heart of creation.

Until we accept full responsibility for all of our thoughts and actions, which impact our Mother the Earth, we remain as children.

By praying to our inside perception, we change the direction of the derision, creating a wave of energy that follows our will.

The madness to create and allow such disasters, both on the waters and on land, is still part of the will and focus of many who need to be overwhelmed with love (so they may forget and leave behind their madness).

When these destructive things are finally left behind, then, and only then, will we begin to experience the benefit of learning our way forward as actualized adults.

Beyond all this is the understanding that only the true Indigenous heart will encompass the energy needed to bond with the earth. Beyond commerce, democracy, feudal law and ego mindedness, there is the truth of our acceptance and love for one another as members of the same endless family.

Each of us, upon reaching this point, will then raise up together, in our collective ability, to release the life-force wave of energy from our hearts; the very energy that is capable of healing and bringing health to humanity.

Readers will be enriched and ennobled by taking to heart, the words and expressions of Michele's true feelings expressed so coherently and forthrightly in the climax of this humbling look at the power of the earth and our own childish neglect of the consequences of our actions.

Martin Carriere (Great White Eagle), author of *Carrying the Chalice Forward and Other Secret Stories of North America*

## You Are Everything ~ Everything Is You

As I undertake my own personal journey, embracing the full impact of learning to improve my life, *You Are Everything: Everything Is You* by author Michele Doucette has spoken *more truths to me*, than any other book I have read to date. Michele provides us with an inspirational message that is relevant to what each of us can do NOW to raise the positive vibration of our planet. This message is further reinforced with an exquisite interweaving of information and quotes from some of the brightest thinkers on the planet, in both scientific and metaphysical approaches.

No doubt you, too, will find reinforcement and clarification of your own truths here; you may even discover new and exciting approaches that can be employed to assist you on your journey to becoming an ever-more enlightened being.

If I could recommend only one book to my friends who have begun their search for greater meaning and purpose in their lives, I would choose this one.

Mariel Barney Hunkeler, Ghost PRO (Paranormal Research Organization)

*You Are Everything: Everything Is You* is a compilation of great material from both the scientific world and that of the spiritual. Packed with well presented information, Michele Doucette has done a fantastic job in putting all this material together.

Camillo Loken, author of *The Shift in Consciousness*

## Cyclic Universe Theory

Scientists are well aware that the universe has exploded into existence, not just once, but repeatedly in endless cycles of death and rebirth; a process that is referred to as cyclic universe theory.

Theoretical physicist, Paul J. Steinhardt, proposes that, courtesy of this theory, [1] space and time may have always existed in an endless cycle of expansion and rebirth; [2] the expansion of the universe is accelerating, as astronomers have recently observed; and [3] after trillions of years, expansion stalls, new matter and radiation is created, and the cycle restarts anew. [17]

This means that "the events that occurred a cycle ago shape our universe today, and the events occurring today will shape our universe a cycle from now. It is this aspect that transforms the metaphysical notion of cycles into a

---

[17] *The Endless Universe: Introduction to the Cyclic Universe* article accessed on March 17, 2011 at http://www.actionbioscience.org/newfrontiers/steinhardt.html

scientifically testable concept. We can make physical measurements today that determine whether the large scale structure of the universe was set before or after the Bang." [18]

It is this particular theory [19] (first introduced in 2002) that "could potentially explain why a mysterious repulsive form of energy known as the *cosmological constant*, and which is accelerating the expansion of the universe, is several orders of magnitude smaller than predicted by the standard Big Bang model," [20] a model that sprung into being 15 billion years ago.

The Big Bang is formally defined "as the moment when the equations say that the temperature and density of the universe became infinite, and it is impossible to extrapolate back any further. Concluding that this represents the

---

[18] Steinhardt, Paul J. and Turok, Neil. (April 2004) *The Cyclic Model Simplified* essay accessed on March 24, 2011 at http://www.physics.princeton.edu/~steinh/dm2004.pdf
[19] Steinhardt, Paul J. and Turok, Neil. (May 2002) *A Cyclic Model of the Universe* research article accessed on March 24, 2011 at http://www.physics.princeton.edu/~steinh/sciencecyc.pdf
[20] *Recycled Mystery: Theory Could Solve Cosmic Mystery* article accessed on March 15, 2011 at http://www.space.com/2372-recycled-universe-theory-solve-cosmic-mystery.html

beginning of all space and time is suspect, however, as Einstein himself once pointed out. Properly construed, finding that the temperature and density become infinite is an indication that the mathematical equations underlying general relativity have become invalid, not that this is when the universe began." [21]

If the superstring theory is proven "to dispel the myth that the Big Bang is the beginning of time" [22] as Paul J. Steinhardt believes, "then it opens up new possibilities for the cosmological history of the Universe." [23]

The cyclic universe theory postulates that the universe has no beginning and no end (in the traditional sense that our 3D minds can comprehend), given that the universe has been exploding into existence, repeatedly over time, extending far into the past as well as into the future.

---

[21] *Does The Universe Repeat Once Every Trillion Years?* Article accessed on March 17, 2011 at
http://seedmagazine.com/content/article/a_cyclic_universe/
[22] *The Endless Universe: Introduction to the Cyclic Universe* article accessed on March 17, 2011 at
http://www.actionbioscience.org/newfrontiers/steinhardt.html
[23] Ibid.

It is quite conceivable, henceforth, that the universe has existed forever.

The cyclic universe theory also states that matter and energy, albeit finite, are infinitely recycled (meaning that energy continues to change form).

The implications of this theory, therefore, are many, meaning ...... [24] [1] that the universe is possibly many times older than we think, [2] that all resources (matter/energy) within the universe are finite, but can be indefinitely recycled through the resetting event, and [3] that such offers an explanation for how the Big Bang occurred and how the universe is continuing in its expansion.

Based on what is referred to as the first law of thermodynamics, a fundamental dictum of physics, we know that energy cannot be destroyed, that it can only be transferred to a new form.

---

[24] *Cyclic Universe Theory* posting accessed on March 15, 2011 at http://www.eve-search.com/thread/1375175/author/Charles%20Baker

It can therefore be concluded that the universe was not created in the way that we understand creation, but that it was merely recycled from energy that cannot be destroyed; likewise for the continual cycles of death and rebirth that are experienced with each new (recycled) incarnation.

Given this fundamental truth, I chanced across a theory referred to as Ducheneism (created by Anthony Duchene in 2011); an argument that uses a recycled energy theory to explain the happenings of the universe.

Believing in the idea that God is not one single person (force), Ducheneism states that while *everything is God, God is also everything*. To put it simply, God is the energy that creates, circulates and becomes recycled. Even though the term recycled is not an overly adequate one, it simply refers to the fact that energy is constantly changing form (which is exactly what we know continues to happen).

As a means of illustrating how energy continues to circulate, when a war has been started, negative energy is created.

Knowing that lives will be lost and widespread famine will be caused, which may well result in increased poverty levels, these particular offshoots demonstrate recycled negative energy (as initially caused by war).

On the flip side, if a person says something nice to you (positive energy), this makes you feel happy (recycled positive energy).

Any further complimentary actions that stem forth from the initial positive energy, as a domino effect that you may have set in motion, can also be referred to as recycled positive energy.

In essence, like attracts like, meaning that what one puts out there is always returned to them.

OK, so far, so good.

Let us now divert to the subject of matter.

Matter is anything made up of atoms and molecules. In addition, matter is anything that has mass.

However, "there is no proof that matter is made of energy. All that can be proven is that matter can be *converted* into energy and vice versa. In fact, you need to have matter to be able to define energy ... one without the other is an oxymoron." [25]

What would life be like, I wonder, without paradoxes, such as these, that keep the head spinning, solely in an attempt to comprehend what comes across, to the greater multitude, as being incomprehensible?

In keeping with Ducheneism, it has been written that while "Jesus may have existed, and was more connected with the earth and its energy, through meditation and so forth, he was not the son of God, as God is not a specific being or object and cannot actually have a son." [26] Instead, God is the energy that is distributed throughout the universe.

---

[25] Philosophy Forums accessed on March 15, 2011 at http://forums.philosophyforums.com/threads/matter-is-not-created-or-destroyed-33846.html

[26] Ducheneism's Views on Jesus Christ posting accessed on March 15, 2011 at http://www.facebook.com/note.php?note_id=168025806574272

In this regard, Jesus was most likely a prophet, a man "who understood that we must feed the Earth positive energy, so that it can distribute positive energy to its subjects." [27]

With God, as pure energy, as universal energy, as *conscious* (fully aware, deliberate and intentional) and *infinite* (boundless and endless) energy, being the sum total of All That Is, the premise put forth, in reference to Ducheneism, is certainly a plausible one.

In connecting with the afterlife, Ducheneism states that "it is believed that every living thing is an energy source. When a person dies, it mostly is a positive event, as much as it is a natural one. The energy that powers the person leaves the body, and is recycled ... with this death comes life; with this positive energy, comes positive effects ... as the energy makeup that is you, is recycled as a different form of energy." [28]

---

[27] Ducheneism's Views on Jesus Christ posting accessed on March 15, 2011 at
http://www.facebook.com/note.php?note_id=168025806574272
[28] Views on Afterlife posting accessed on March 15, 2011 at
http://www.facebook.com/note.php?note_id=168037566573096

Knowing that energy is incarnate, that energy is constant, that energy is cyclical, that everything emanates from the same source, I am everything and everything is me. Likewise, you *are* everything and everything *is* you; hence, the aptness of the title of this book.

If we come to understand and believe that I am you and you are me, despite the fact that *we appear to be separated only in order to experience individuality*, surely this gives one pause to think things through, with clarity and intent, before uttering threats and words of defamation, and/or displaying actions of ill intent, toward another.

All of us need to begin thinking of ourselves in this same light: we are every bit as big as the sun, the earth, the stars, the planets and all the universes combined, simply because we are made of the same stuff.

## The Unified Field

The unified field, according to modern physics, is "the deepest, most powerful level of Nature's functioning, and the source of the infinite creativity and intelligence within every individual and displayed throughout the universe." [29]

Gregg Braden, in <u>The Divine Matrix</u>, talks about the universe having been founded on four characteristics; namely, [1] that there is a field of energy that connects all of creation (discovery 1); [2] that this field takes on the role of a container, a bridge and a mirror for the beliefs as held by the individual (discovery 2); [3] that this field is nonlocal and holographic, meaning that every part of it is connected to another, with each piece mirroring the whole on a smaller scale (discovery 3); and [4] that we communicate with this field through the language of emotion (discovery 4). [30]

---

[29] The Unified Field: The Key to Enlightenment, National Invincibility and World Peace website accessed on March 16, 2011 at http://www.america.unifiedfieldconferences.org/

[30] Braden, Gregg. (2007). *The Divine Matrix: Bridging Time, Space, Miracles and Belief* (page xxi). Carlsbad, CA: Hay House, Inc.

Gregg Braden is not the first to suggest that coherent emotion is the language that this field of energy understands; Esther and Jerry Hicks, through the words of Abraham, feel the same way.

Coherent emotion "happens when what we are thinking, feeling, and expressing are all in alignment." [31]

Of course, this means that incoherent emotion can be described as "the kind of emotion we experience when we are feeling one way, thinking another way, and expressing something different from either our thoughts or our feelings." [32]

When you think about something, further coupled with feelings and emotions, you are sending out powerful vibrations.

Everything is connected, meaning that your vibrations affect everyone, directly or indirectly.

---

[31] *Oneness and The Unified Field* article accessed on March 16. 2011 at http://www.escapetheillusion.com/blog/2008/10/oneness-and-the-unified-field-gregg-braden/
[32] Ibid.

## You Are Everything ~ Everything Is You

Everything you do (what you are thinking, what you are feeling, what you say, how you behave) is vibrated into the universal field (universal consciousness) of which you are a significant particle of source energy.

Knowing that each is affected by the other (directly or indirectly, as mentioned previously) is what demonstrates the interconnectivity (transpersonal consciousness) that exists between all of us.

In keeping with the unified field (with other names being Consciousness, Consciousness Grid, Source of Creation, Oneness, Unity, Nature's Mind, Mind of God and Quantum Hologram, to cite but a few), you are part of God. God is in you, as well as everywhere.

This means that "we are not simply a part of the Earth; we *are* the Earth. We are not simply a part of the Force that governs all Creation; we *are* that Force." [33]

---

[33] Bolsta, Phil. (2009). *Gregg Braden on Prayer and the Unified Field* posting accessed on March 16, 2011 at http://bolstablog.wordpress.com/2009/12/06/braden-video/

Consciousness, then, can be said to originate from the very fabric of this unified field.

It is this experience of consciousness, this utilization of what consciousness and the unified field means, that leads to increased intelligence, increased creativity, better health, decreased anxiety, increased self-actualization and better job performance, all of which serve to further enhance continued and increased successfulness in all avenues of one's life.

If these same experiences were to take place on an ever increasing collective level, such would lead to enhanced coherence and harmony (meaning that there would be less instances of both domestic as well as international conflict) among nations. [34]

In 1960, Maharishi Mahesh Yogi predicted that one percent of a population practicing the Transcendental Meditation

---

[34] *Unified Field of All the Laws of Nature* article accessed on March 17, 2011 at
http://worldpeaceendowment.org/invincibility/invincibility7.html

technique would produce measurable improvements in the quality of life for the whole population.

This phenomenon, known as the Maharishi Effect, was first noticed in 1974 and reported in a paper published in 1976. The findings were such that "when 1% of a community practiced the Transcendental Meditation® program, the crime rate was reduced by 16% on average." [35]

The basis of the Maharishi Effect is the rise in collective consciousness, meaning "the wholeness of consciousness of any specific group. For example, when we talk of community consciousness, we merely put together the consciousness of all the individuals who make up the community; for national consciousness we put together the consciousness of all the citizens of a nation." [36]

---

[35] Maharishi University of Management website. *Research on the Maharishi Effect* article accessed on March 28, 2011 at http://www.mum.edu/m_effect/
[36] Maharishi Vedic University (1999) website. *The Maharishi Effect* article accessed on March 17, 2011 at http://www.vedicknowledge.com/Maharishi_effect.html

Since the theory and the phenomenon are so new to modern science, "the methodology of a study is subjected to rigorous analysis by the journal review boards before a paper on the Maharishi Effect is accepted for publication." [37]

In keeping with the Maharishi Effect, Dr. David Edwards, Professor of Government, at the University of Texas, has been referenced as saying ... "I think the claim can be plausibly made that the potential impact of this research exceeds that of any other ongoing social or psychological research program. It has survived a broader array of statistical tests than most research in the field of conflict resolution. This work and the theory that informs it deserve the most serious consideration by academics and policy makers alike." [38]

---

[37] Maharishi Vedic University (1999) website. *The Maharishi Effect* article accessed on March 17, 2011 at http://www.vedicknowledge.com/Maharishi_effect.html
[38] Maharishi University of Management website. *Research on the Maharishi Effect* article accessed on March 28, 2011 at http://www.mum.edu/m_effect/

In this sense, we operate very much like radio transmitters and receivers, sending out signals (vibrations), courtesy of the electromagnetic field that surrounds us.

In returning to the words of Gregg Braden, at the opening of this particular chapter, as individuals, we are constantly creating effects on every part of creation because it is consciousness that permeates every aspect of the unified field.

Many of us have taken the time, at some point in our lives, to throw a stone into a pond. It is this motion that creates ripples that spread outward. As miniscule as we may believe ourselves to be, it is in a fashion similar to this that we are actually able to transform the cosmos.

Since collective consciousness "is created by the individuals within it, as individual consciousness grows, collective consciousness rises; and as collective consciousness rises, individual consciousness grows. In other words, as an individual regularly experiences self-referral consciousness and enlivens it in his own awareness, the levels of collective consciousness in which he participates (family, city, province, nation, etc.) are simultaneously improved. This higher value of collective consciousness, in turn, effects, in a positive way, every one of the individual members of that level of collective consciousness." [39]

The unified field of consciousness is "the essence and source of creation of everyone, regardless of race, age, gender, background, richness or poverty; place and time. Whatever we individually think, experience or believe, we are all conscious beings sharing the same essence." [40]

However, it becomes the beliefs that we have about ourselves, the beliefs to which we have become ingrained and attached, that create the sense of separation that is felt. Clearly, *we are the source of our own perceived limitations.*

The language of this energy field, as shared earlier, appears to be coherent emotion, which is what creates a chemical

---

[39] Maharishi Vedic University (1999) website. *The Maharishi Effect* article accessed on March 17, 2011 at http://www.vedicknowledge.com/Maharishi_effect.html

[40] The Unified Field – The Consciousness of All Creation website accessed on March 17, 2011 at http://www.anunda.com/paradigm/unified-field.htm

shift (in the pH levels) within our bodies. In addition, the hormonal levels in the body are also changed.

For example, "the life-affirming hormone precursor DHEA increases over 100 percent in our bodies in the space of only six hours in the presence of coherent emotions of appreciation and gratitude." [41]

By comparison, "life-depleting hormones like cortisol, the stress hormone, decrease over 23 percent in that same six hours in the presence of incoherent emotion." [42]

Measureable statements such as these are truly indicative of the body having the potential to heal itself. There is much to be said for emotional energy.

Michael Sky, author of <u>The Power of Emotion: Using Your Emotional Energy to Transform Your Life</u>, defines emotion as *energy in motion*, a most apt term.

---

[41] *Oneness and The Unified Field* article accessed on March 16. 2011 at http://www.escapetheillusion.com/blog/2008/10/oneness-and-the-unified-field-gregg-braden/
[42] Ibid.

When you suppress emotion, you are not living; instead, you are merely existing within, what some might term, a meager sense of presence.

Over time "most people develop strategies for feeling less. Since emotion vexes and torments us so, we find ways to suppress our emotional experience. We learn to deaden our feelings, to turn off sensation, to numb out. Like rocks in the midst of rushing water – unmoved and unmovable – we cultivate stoicism. We strive to prevail, unaffected by life's changes. Those who never show their feelings reap the highest praise." [43]

Now that is a most scary thought – that to be feeling dead on the inside, as well as the outside, is what reaps the highest praise (simply because you never let your feelings show). Not a life, in the truest sense, one is merely eking out an existence, if, indeed, that is even the proper term.

---

[43] Sky, Michael. *The Power of Emotion: Using Your Emotional Energy to Transform Your Life* (page 2). Rochester, VT: Bear & Company.

As a general rule, most tend to rationalize and analyze, in a clearheaded and logical fashion, making sure that they always maintain control of their emotions. This is what defines maturity, they say.

They learn to distrust anything that involves emotional involvement, not wanting to become engaged in that manner. Knowing that this is what reaps the highest praise, if I may once again reiterate, is downright scary.

That so many people "do so well at suppressing their emotions constitutes a singular failing in human development;" [44] a failing that has become a significant part of the collective consciousness to which we all belong.

How can one begin the process of self-healing, if everything is suppressed, if everything is denied, if everything is buried?

---

[44] Sky, Michael. *The Power of Emotion: Using Your Emotional Energy to Transform Your Life* (page 3). Rochester, VT: Bear & Company.

## You Are Everything ~ Everything Is You

We are privileged to live in a world that has been infused with a vital, living, conscious, infinite, fluid (meaning malleable) energy. As vital, living, conscious and infinite beings, capable of change, we, too, are this same energy.

Life experiences are created by beliefs, imaginations, and emotions, all of which work together as one system. Emotions (energy in motion), however, are the link that exists between the body, mind and spirit; an affiliation that must now be forged anew.

It is imperative that you learn to analyze (in a detached way) and challenge your beliefs. It is equally as important that you detach yourself from the hardened belief systems that continue to generate superstition, bias, discrimination, bigotry, intolerance, chauvinism, prejudice, ignorance, irrationality and premature (and sometimes perverse) conclusions. Learning to release yourself from these negative outcomes is what shall begin to transform your inner world.

As you work toward attaining the inner peace (emotional freedom) that is needed, you are achieving self-healing.

## You Are Everything ~ Everything Is You

Remembering that as individual consciousness grows, so, too, does this affect the collective consciousness in a positive way.

Anything that one does to enhance their lives in the here and now, can only serve to also benefit the unified field to which all are connected.

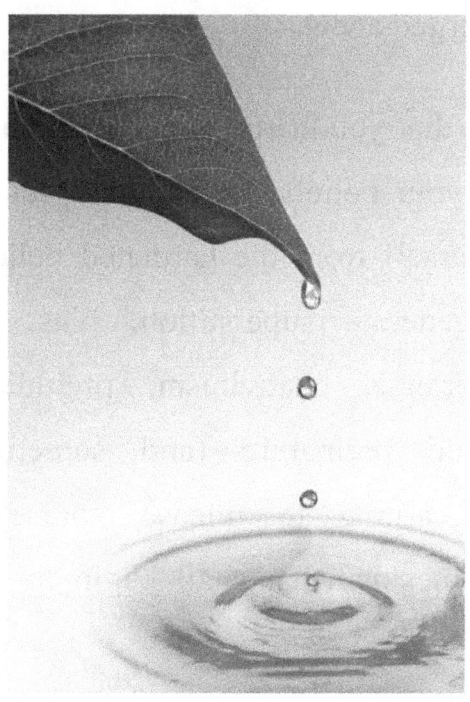

# Vedic Science of Consciousness

It was in the course of researching the Maharishi Effect that I came across the term Vedic Science of Consciousness.

Vedic Science pertains to the Vedas. The Vedas are a large body of texts, long preserved in ancient India, that constitute the oldest authority of Sanskrit literature. They are also the oldest Hindu scriptures.

The Vedic tradition "includes detailed information on a wide range of topics: from astronomy to music, architecture to health care, administration to economy. But it is all based on the knowledge of consciousness, including technologies of consciousness, and evolution to the highest state of consciousness (enlightenment)." [45]

Is it possible, then, that this Vedic (pronounced VAY-dik) tradition might be the most ancient source of knowledge

---

[45] *The Vedic Tradition* article accessed on March 17, 2011 at http://www.permanentpeace.org/source/tradition.html

(with respect to both consciousness and meditation) that we currently have access to?

Modern science coupled with ancient wisdom is something that I find fascinating. As a result of having contributed to this profound body of knowledge, Maharishi Mahesh Yogi (affiliated with the Maharishi Effect as discussed in the previous chapter) is "widely recognized as the world's foremost Vedic scholar, as well as its leading scientist of consciousness." [46]

To transcend means [1] *to rise above or go beyond* as well as [2] *to outdo, exceed or surpass in excellence, elevation, extent or degree.*

Transcendental Consciousness, then, means moving from one level of mental activity to another. In truth, Transcendental Consciousness means going from the active level of the mind (whereby there are constant thoughts) to the non-active (silent) level of the mind.

---

[46] *The Founder* article accessed on March 18, 2011 at http://www.permanentpeace.org/source/founder.html

However, the difference between sleep and Transcendental Consciousness is that the latter refers to *being aware of the inner silence that has been reached within the awake state*; a state which is vastly different from sleep.

Transcendental Meditation is but one possible technique that enables an individual to experience, first-hand, this inner silence.

Thoughts create "boundaries in the mind; by experiencing thoughts all day long, your mind experiences only boundaries. If [on the other hand] you regularly experience Transcendental Consciousness through Transcendental Meditation, your mind gains the ability to experience both thoughts and the silent source of all thoughts at the same time ... [enabling you] to experience both boundaries and unboundedness." [47]

It is this very unboundedness that presents itself as both total freedom and complete expansion.

---

[47] *What is Transcendental Consciousness?* article accessed on March 19, 2011 at
http://www.transcendentalconsciousness.com/transcending.htm

Research is showing that continued Transcendental Consciousness cognizance results in less stress, a stronger immune system, better resistance against disease, and more energy. In addition, you are also able to maintain a much more broad focus (through a sense of emotional detachment), all of which enables you to make better decisions with respect to difficult situations. It is within this most silent state of human awareness (a state of restful alertness and inner peace), that one experiences the unified field (also referred to as the physical field of peace).

The experience of Transcendental Consciousness is said to be profound, thereby allowing "the mind to experience the deepest level of its *own* intelligence, which is described as the deepest level of the intelligence displayed everywhere in nature – the unified field of all the laws of nature. The technology of transcending thus allows the individual mind to align itself with all the laws of nature at their source." [48]

---

[48] *Transcendental Consciousness Defined* article accessed on March 19, 2011 at http://www.permanentpeace.org/technology/tc.html

As one repeatedly experiences the unified field, courtesy of Transcendental Consciousness, "the human mind and body rapidly evolve toward higher levels of functioning," [49] a fact that has been successfully demonstrated in more than 600 scientific studies, published in many of the world's leading scientific journals.

Modern science is beginning to catch up with ancient wisdom. In fact, both physicists and physiologists have been able to validate "timeless Vedic understandings of both the natural world and human consciousness" [50] meaning that "nature and human nature are united at their source." [51]

Quantum field theories tell us that the unified field is a field of pure intelligence, the very source of the entire natural world as we know it.

This unified field is also "an abstract, nonmaterial field that can be directly contacted (and experienced) by the human

---

[49] *Transcendental Consciousness Defined* article accessed on March 19, 2011 at http://www.permanentpeace.org/technology/tc.html
[50] *Creating Peace: Four Central Concepts* article accessed on March 19, 2011 at http://www.permanentpeace.org/theory/peace.html#3
[51] Ibid.

mind" [52] through Transcendental Consciousness, meaning that it is within "this state of least excitation of human consciousness, this state of inner peace ... [that] the mind gains access to the limitless intelligence of nature." [53]

As demonstrated in the Vedic literature, Transcendental Consciousness (during which time there is a direct experience of the unified field of natural law) is referred to as the fourth major state of consciousness. "This profound state of inner peace is known in Sanskrit as *samadhi* (unwavering mind), or simply *turiya* (the fourth)." [54]

When groups of individuals experience Transcendental Consciousness together, a "powerful influence of peace radiates into the entire society. Fifty demonstration projects and 23 published studies have identified this radiating influence of peace, as measured by reduced crime, accidents,

---

[52] *Creating Peace: Four Central Concepts* article accessed on March 19, 2011 at http://www.permanentpeace.org/theory/peace.html#3
[53] Ibid.
[54] *Transcendental Consciousness Objectively Verified* article accessed on March 19, 2011 at
http://www.permanentpeace.org/technology/verified.html

warfare, and terrorism." [55] James Twyman, Gregg Braden and Doreen Virtue have also been involved in many peace projects that have been scientifically shown to generate the same.

Transcendental Meditation is a technique that is "based on the ancient Vedic tradition of enlightenment in India. This knowledge has been handed down by Vedic masters from generation to generation for thousands of years. About 50 years ago, Maharishi, the representative in our age of the Vedic tradition, introduced Transcendental Meditation to the world, restoring the knowledge and experience of higher states of consciousness at this critical time for humanity." [56]

It was Camillo Løken, webmaster of One Mind: One Energy, [57] who introduced me to the Natural Stress Relief meditation technique. [58]

---

[55] *Creating Peace: Four Central Concepts* article accessed on March 19, 2011 at http://www.permanentpeace.org/theory/peace.html#3
[56] Maharishi Vedic Education Development Corporation (2010). *The Transcendental Meditation Program* accessed on March 19, 2011 at http://www.maharishi.ca/
[57] http://www.one-mind-one-energy.com/

Learning to activate this unified field of peace and bliss, courtesy of Transcendental Consciousness (by whichever means are comfortable, easily accessible and/or available), shows us that world peace is very much achievable.

---

[58] http://www.naturalstressreliefusa.org/

# The Proof

The saints and mystics were unanimous in their belief that we are not the separate beings we believe ourselves to be, but that we are, in reality, one. James Twyman, renowned author and crusader for peace, together with co-author and spiritual teacher Anakha Coman, have found a way to prove, once and for all, that separation is an illusion.

There is a bond that exists between us, an unseen link that unites us in ways that nothing else can. *You are here to know yourself to be one with the totality of all creation* (the unified field) *and everything that exists*; it is this experience that expands the field of opportunity on a significantly profound level.

In truth, oneness is not something that can be described in words; it can only be realized through direct experience.

Steve Pavlina identifies three different ways of relating to humanity; namely, [1] self-centeredness, [2] neutrality and [3] oneness.

At the level of self-centeredness, you are completely focused on serving the self, pursuing your own advancement at the expense of others. "Others will only connect with you because they feel they have to or because they can gain something from it. This means your connections with other people are basically reduced to the level of transactions. They are loveless and devoid of deeper meaning." [59] Living a life of self-centeredness is what leads to a life of disconnection, a life whereby individuals are able to watch the suffering of others with no sense of caring or compassion.

It becomes during the neutrality phase that one adopts the mantra of *live and let live*, a phrase that many are familiar with. This, then, becomes a case of making sure that you do not do harm to another. It also means that you are not going out of your way to do something good for that person, either. There are no intentions other than living your life (while harming none) and letting others live theirs, all just to get by on a day-to-day basis.

---

[59] Pavlina, Steve. (2008) *Oneness* article accessed on March 19, 2011 at http://www.stevepavlina.com/blog/2008/10/oneness/

The difficulty, herein, is that "if there are other self-centered people at large in the body of humanity, then your attitude of neutrality actually contributes to the problem." [60] Considered the least powerful path, this is where the majority of humanity finds themselves. "If you're neutral, it's a safe bet that much of your life is controlled by others. This is the place of living reactively instead of proactively. Even when you set goals, they're likely to be socially conditioned ones, and most likely you won't feel strongly empowered by them." [61]

Before continuing any further, I wish to state that while I address the concept of emotional detachment in my other spiritual and metaphysical volumes, neutrality is a completely different concept. When I speak of emotional detachment, I am not referring to an inability to connect with others in an emotional fashion. Instead, I am referencing a mental assertiveness (a positive and deliberate mental attitude) that allows one to disengage their emotions related

---

[60] Pavlina, Steve. (2008) *Oneness* article accessed on March 19, 2011 at http://www.stevepavlina.com/blog/2008/10/oneness/
[61] Ibid.

to others (so as not to be unnecessarily manipulated) while still maintaining a level of empathy and compassion. Neutrality, as described by Steve Pavlina, is a completely different state.

We finally arrive at the third option – to live with the attitude of oneness. "Oneness is the logical and emotional recognition that we're all part of the same whole and that we aren't separate from each other. We're all cells in the larger body of humanity. Its fate is our fate. If the body suffers, we all suffer for it. If the body thrives, we all benefit from it." [62] When you fully internalize this mindset and commit yourself to it, "something rather magical happens. The larger body recognizes your commitment to service, and it actively seeks to assist you. By helping you, the body is simply helping itself." [63]

Steve writes about an activity that he terms *Oneness World* whereby individuals are asked to take ten minutes each day to sit quietly and relax, all in an effort to imagine what it

---

[62] Pavlina, Steve. (2008) *Oneness* article accessed on March 19, 2011 at http://www.stevepavlina.com/blog/2008/10/oneness/
[63] Ibid.

would be like to live in a world that is in total alignment with oneness; a world where all people feel joyful and connected with everyone else; a world where cooperation replaces competition; a world where "we" thinking replaces "me" thinking; a world where profiting at someone else's expense never happens; a world where everyone assumes personal responsibility for the well-being of everyone else.

In this world of oneness, "you can always expect fair treatment, regardless of race, gender, or sexual preference. If you need help with anything, you can approach anyone at any time, and you'll be treated like family. The very notion of individual advancement at the expense of others is completely alien. This world's mantra is: *We're all in this together*." [64]

Likewise, in this new world, there are "no weapons, no prisons, and no national borders. There's no violence or war. People still have differences of opinion, but they settle them

---

[64] Pavlina, Steve. (2008) *Personal Power for Smart People* (as taken from Chapter 4). Carlsbad, CA: Hay House, Inc.

by cooperating to discover the truth while treating every individual with compassion and fairness." [65]

One must take the time to allow their mind and emotions to roam freely through this *Oneness World* activity. It is imperative that you think about what it would be like to actually live there, paying close attention to how it makes you feel.

Should you take the time to participate in this exercise, you will find yourself experiencing some of these visualized benefits as you begin to align yourself with oneness. "When you interact with others from a place of cooperation, fairness, and compassion, you'll tend to receive similar treatment in return. When you treat everyone as a friend or family member, you'll often find them responding in kind. Over time, you'll attract others who resonate with oneness, which will enable you to create a microcosm of the larger ideal within your own life." [66]

---

[65] Pavlina, Steve. (2008) *Personal Power for Smart People* (as taken from Chapter 4). Carlsbad, CA: Hay House, Inc.
[66] Ibid.

As shared by a dear friend of mine, while this fantasy world deepens our understanding of oneness, the most important aspect missing (in this exercise) is the role that money has played in our lives.

For this Utopian world to become a reality (and it is my sincere belief that it can), it must be taken one step further in that money must be removed.

Money, as a form of energy exchange, is inherently good; however, it is easy to see that money has become a tool by which to promote greed, corruption and crime (all of which merely serve to further divide humanity).

If we are to successfully return to the Golden Age, a time in which all can choose to work at a job that each feels passionate about, but without monetary retribution of any kind, perhaps we must return to a barter type system once more; a system in which goods or services are directly exchanged for other goods and/or services. In this way, all come to feel a sense of achievement, a sense of fulfillment, a sense of recompense, for the activity is which they are engaged.

Clearly, as increasingly more individuals embrace this particular philosophy of life, making these integral changes in their own lives, the better life becomes for all of us.

In short, given the current state of the larger body of humanity, "it isn't enough to do no harm. You must also proactively commit yourself to doing good. *Allowing harm to be done is just as irresponsible as causing direct harm.* Our inherent interconnectedness is undeniable." [67]

It is this approach that aids in the healing of the wounded self. It is also this same approach that allows you to remain in complete alignment with truth and love.

In adopting the mindset of oneness, we are actively supported. "When we need help, there's a knock on the door with an offer of assistance. When we need resources, they freely flow to us. When we need ideas, they come to us." [68]

---

[67] Pavlina, Steve. (2008) *Oneness* article accessed on March 19, 2011 at http://www.stevepavlina.com/blog/2008/10/oneness/
[68] Ibid.

When we totally oppose and/or resist this mindset, we experience both indifference (aloofness, carelessness and disregard) as well as resistance (conditional antagonism).

Your "degree of alignment (or misalignment) with oneness is a statement of your basic approach to living as a human being. Aligning yourself with oneness makes life easier on so many levels. It transforms resistance into acceptance, competition into cooperation, and sorrow into joy." [69]

Oneness translates to oneness with self, with others, with God (aka the unified field of intelligence and consciousness); it is an awakening to the universal truths that reside within.

Oneness is a process that also involves learning to be conscious, learning to live within the moment, without judgment, without any preconceived ideas about what should be.

---

[69] Pavlina, Steve. (2008) *Oneness* article accessed on March 19, 2011 at http://www.stevepavlina.com/blog/2008/10/oneness/

## You Are Everything ~ Everything Is You

The teachings of Buddha are referred to as the Noble Eight Fold Path. The first step, *samyag-drsti* in Sanskrit, usually translates to Right Understanding.

Ian Paul Marshall prefers to use the words Perfect Vision instead because it is indicative of "something that is transformative on an individual level." [70]

It is courtesy of this very transformation that you awaken to a new paradigm, a new ideal, a new prototype for yourself, in that you are finally able to see that your thoughts, words, actions and deeds are what have continued to contribute to the collective whole (be they positive or otherwise).

When you are able to see that your world is the way it is, simply because you have made it thusly, you have arrived at what becomes the impetus that is needed for awakening.

---

[70] Marshall, Ian Paul. *Global Awakening – What Does That Really Mean?* article accessed on March 19, 2011 at http://ianpaulmarshall.com/global-awakening-what-does-that-really-mean/

This becomes the point whereby you begin to develop a deep and inner awareness of the natural laws of the universe; the first step towards oneness.

In the context of relationships, oneness "means accepting people as they are, without wanting them to be different. It means letting go of expectations and viewing their personalities or actions as neither superior nor inferior. It means simply knowing people as they are, and accepting them in totality." [71]

This next segment, as also shared by Valerie Brooks, is crucial.

People "are our mirrors. We love or hate people because of what we respectively admire or despise in ourselves. If I can accept another person, I am ultimately accepting myself." [72]

---

[71] Brooks, Valerie. (2001) *Oneness and Tantra* article accessed on March 19, 2011 at
http://www.innerself.com/content/relationships/sexuality/general/4039-oneness-a-tantra.html
[72] Ibid.

While I have addressed this same concept in previous works, I appreciate how Valerie's words come together because it becomes in total acceptance of the self that you are also contributing to your own self healing.

In adopting the mindset of oneness, do not expect it to be an easy venture; likewise, do not expect it to be an instantaneous happening. It is my inherent wish, however, that the world will awaken to this mindset of connectedness.

## The Power Lies Within

According to the Kybalion, a book dedicated to Hermetic philosophy (which claims to be the essence of the teachings of Hermes Trismegistus) and published in 1912, there are seven universal laws, the first one being the Principle of Mentalism. This law references the fact that all is mind, meaning that, so, too, is the universe an infinite, conscious, living mind.

The American poet, Ralph Waldo Emerson (1803 – 1882), understanding the oneness of creation, believed that we should do our best to live simply (in harmony) with both nature as well as each other. Living in harmony does not mean polluting the oceans, polluting the air and/or ravaging the earth by way of mining, blasting and the use of radioactive materials.

Quantum physics states that substance comes into existence through actual observation, meaning that when a mind thinks something into existence, it becomes real.

Thus, *energy is both conscious* (fully aware, deliberate and intentional) *and infinite* (boundless and endless).

Consciousness is an extension of mind, meaning that we can literally *think something into existence*. If we create using mind in this manner, then, so, too, is mind reality, is it not?

All energy "is influenced by thought and structures itself into taking form as an observable effect. Everything that happens, has happened and will happen in the entire universe, first originated as a thought originating from the Mind of a Being, which in turn has its corresponding effect on energy and becomes a corresponding and potentially observable affect." [73]

The act of focusing your consciousness is also an act of creation, meaning that consciousness creates.

Everything you are witness to in your own life was, first and foremost, a thought. This is why it becomes so absolutely crucial to become aware of what you think.

---

[73] Tan, Enoch. *The Nature of All Reality and The Universal Construct* article (February 2006).

Thinking positive thoughts and demonstrating positive emotions (feelings) means that you are sending out positive vibrations. Knowing that like attracts like, so, too, will these positive emanations be returned to you.

The same also holds for negative thoughts and emotions (feelings). Taking it one step further, in truth, a negative thought or feeling about someone else will only end up hurting you, as well, given the fact that we are all connected.

You become what you think about; hence, believing in yourself is key. It is possible to use your mind, and your thoughts, to achieve the goals that you have set for yourself.

If you can envision it, you can do it. It is equally as important, however, that you also take steps of action towards this anticipated achievement.

Taking the time to complete the necessary mind work is not easy, requiring much diligence and effort.

You need to practice how to be positive.

You need to practice believing in yourself.

You need to believe that you can do anything that you put your mind to.

This is the power of thought applied in a positive way.

Everything about you can change from one moment to the next (thoughts, feelings and emotions), depending on what your consciousness is focused upon.

Your emotions determine the effectiveness of your actions. Negative states only serve to make you feel increasingly stuck, whereas positive states are empowering. Spending time with supportive and positive people helps keep one positive.

Affirmations have been proven to work for those who feel and believe in the words (messages) they are reciting to themselves. While affirmations can be utilized throughout the day, they are <u>even more effective</u> if stated *before you go to sleep* given the fact that brain activity slows down when you are entering the Alpha brainwave level (the necessary level for reprogramming and rewiring your brain), a state of physical and mental relaxation.

In conjunction with creative visualization, the power of thought can be used to manifest dreams and create change.

It is important to remember that no one thinks the exact same thoughts the way you do; hence, there is no one that sends out the exact same vibrational frequencies that you do. I was incredibly excited to see this described as a *mental fingerprint*, [74] meaning that everything connected to you is unique.

Thoughts and ideas are energy. They are the building blocks of creation. One must first have the thought before it can be manifested into form. To have the thought, one must first have mind.

All of creation (meaning form) is the product of mind and thought; hence, all of creation is the product of imagination. Mind, therefore, can be said to be the very catalyst behind everything in existence.

As a result, we are limited only by our imaginations.

---

[74] http://www.one-mind-one-energy.com/unique.html

Every thought you have, has the power to influence events in either a positive or negative way. Your thoughts and beliefs create situations. What you experience is up to you.

In essence, life is clearly what you *imagine* it to be.

Thomas Troward (1847 – 1916) was an English author with a special interest in mental science. His writing heavily influenced what is called the New Thought movement.

*If I were asked what, in my opinion, distinguishes the thought of the present day from that of a previous generation, I should feel inclined to say, it is the fact that people are beginning to realize that Thought is a power in itself, one of the great forces of the Universe, and ultimately the greatest of forces, directing all the others. Thought is the great power of the Universe. But to make it practically available we must know something of the principles by which it works – that it is not a mere vaporous indefinable influence floating around and subject to no known laws, but that on the contrary, it follows laws as uncompromising as those of mathematics, while at the same time allowing unlimited freedom to the individual.*

These words come from his book, <u>The Law and the Word</u>, published in 1917.  Genevieve Behrend, a personal student of Thomas Troward, was the author of both <u>Your Invisible Power</u> as well as <u>Attaining Your Desires</u>.

More than 100 years ago, Wallace D. Wattles wrote <u>The Science of Getting Rich</u>.  In writing these words ... *there is a thinking stuff from which all things are made, and which, in its original state, permeates, penetrates, and fills the interspaces of the universe* ... it seems clear that he was talking about the unified field.

You already have all the power you need to create all of the changes that you wish for yourself.  It is the focus of your awareness (mindfulness) that will become the reality of your world.

Change can only begin from within.

It was William James, a Harvard Psychologist, and the touted Father of American Psychology, that said ... *The greatest discovery of the 19th century was not in the realm of the physical sciences, but the power of the subconscious mind touched by faith. Any individual can tap into an eternal reservoir of power that will enable them to overcome any problem that may arise. All weaknesses can be overcome (bodily healing, financial independence, spiritual awakening, prosperity) beyond your wildest dreams. This is the superstructure of happiness.* [75]

There are four brainwave pattern categories: Beta, Alpha, Theta and Delta. Each of these brainwave patterns are associated with specific states and serve important functions.

Beta waves are quick waves of 13 to 30 times per second (Hz). Beta brainwave patterns are generated naturally when we are awake and alert.

Alpha waves exist between 8 and 12 Hz. Alpha waves usually occur during rest (when the eyes are closed), intellectual relaxation, deep relaxation, meditation or when calming the mind; the desired result of experienced meditators.

---

[75] http://visionandwords.com/2011/02/26/words-by-william-jamesthe-harvard-psychologist-known-as-the-father-of-american-psychology/

Those who can remain in the Alpha level while analyzing information also have access to more information through intuition, creative ideas and inspirational thoughts.

Theta waves exist between 4 and 7 Hz. Commonly referred to as the dream or "twilight" state, Theta is associated with learning, memory, REM sleep and dreaming.

Memory development is enhanced while in the Theta state. Likewise, memory is improved (especially long term memory), and access to unconscious material, reveries, free association, insights and creative ideas is increased.

Delta brainwave patterns usually occur when we are asleep. Delta waves, ranging from .5 to 3 Hz, are the slowest.

While our mental state affects our brainwaves, the opposite is also true, meaning that *our brainwaves affect our mental state*.

This means that we can actually control our mental state by controlling our brainwaves.

In addition, doctors have found that a patient can trigger self-healing by the *mere belief that they will be cured*. This is commonly called the placebo effect.

There is no explanation for why the placebo effect works, except that somehow the belief of the patient, that they are being cured, triggers some sort of self-healing ability. The placebo effect is probably the best documented way in which the mind is known to affect the body. On the flip side, if you believe that something is harmful to you, it tends to become so.

In summation, your mind is your most potent tool in your quest for a healthy body and soul.

In words as spoken by Dr. David Felten (University of Rochester School of Medicine) ... *We can no longer pretend that the patient's perceptions don't matter. And we can't pretend that healing is something doctors do to a patient. Your mind is in every cell of your body. And your emotions are the bridge between the mental and the physical, or the physical and the mental. It's either way. Now there is overwhelming evidence that hormones and neurotransmitters can influence the activities of the immune system, and that products of the immune system can influence the brain.* [76]

The secret, it seems, lies in employing strategies (like meditation and visualization, among others) within the Alpha state, while also remembering that there are surges of intuition (that enable the access of significant knowledge and wisdom) that is being received at this level of brainwave activity.

It was Albert Einstein who said ... *There are only two ways to live your life. One is as if nothing is a miracle, and the other is as if everything is a miracle.*

Clearly, there is inherent truth to be found within these words.

---

[76] http://www.suestar.com/resources/res_mind_body.html

# Mindfulness

Learning to live in the moment (in the now) is not as difficult as many make it out to be.

When you are feeling agitated and upset, stop and take the time to breathe. When you are feeling angry and frustrated, stop and take the time to breathe. When you are feeling disillusioned and depressed, stop and take the time to breathe.

We allow ourselves so little time to practice stillness and calm. Taking the time to breathe, while placing your whole focus on the breath, is taking a much needed step in the right direction.

It was Buddha who shared …… *All that we are is the result of what we have thought. The mind is everything. What we think, we become.*

In truth, while we are *not* our thoughts, we have come to believe that we are.

Most of us "don't undertake our thoughts in awareness. Rather, our thoughts control us. *Ordinary thoughts course through our mind like a deafening waterfall,* writes Jon Kabat-Zinn, the biomedical scientist who introduced meditation into mainstream medicine. *In order to feel more in control of our minds and our lives, to find the sense of balance that eludes us, we need to step out of this current, to pause, and,* as Kabat-Zinn puts it, *to rest in stillness – to stop doing and focus on just being."* [77]

Living in the moment is also called mindfulness, an active and operative state of focusing solely on the present.

It was Norman Vincent Peale who coined the term *Infinite Possibilitarian*. It is now time to wake up to the fact that anything is possible in each moment; that each of us can become that infinite possibilitarian. As you encounter perceived limitations on your path, know that these illusions are merely there to awaken you.

---

[77] Dixit, Jay. (2008) *The Art of Now: Six Steps to Living in the Moment* article accessed on March 21, 2011 at http://www.psychologytoday.com/articles/200810/the-art-now-six-steps-living-in-the-moment

It is in the welcoming of these perceived limitations that one can rediscover a much bigger universe than they ever dreamed possible.

It is this simple shift in thinking that will expand your consciousness, allowing you to see possibilities in life where once you thought you were stuck.

What you are thinking and feeling (or vibrating) right now has a definite and direct impact on your immediate future.

That having been said, you are *not* your thoughts and you are *not* your feelings, despite the fact that they are an integral part of the physical experience.

Transcending the mind is akin to *watching* your thoughts and feelings pass by, choosing which thought and/or feeling to entertain at any given moment.

Whatever influences the mind also affects the body. All diseases get into the body by way of the mind, courtesy of persistent and continued mental tension and worry. Unfortunately, most are unaware of this profound truth.

In keeping, it has been said that the mind can either be the cause of one's bondage or the cause of one's liberation.

Negative thoughts beget bondage.

Positive thoughts beget liberation.

While stilling the chatter of the mind can aid in mental and physical relaxation, what is even more important is recognizing and acknowledging that you are *not* your mind.

Transcending the dualistic mind is the battle of surrendering the bullying of the mind (ego dominated existence) to mindfulness (awareness of one's thoughts, actions and motivations).

Mindfulness means *being aware of the moment in which we are living*.

Mindfulness is *meditation in action*, allowing life to unfold without the limitation of prejudgment.

Mindfulness means *being open to an awareness*, whilst *becoming that Infinite Possibilitarian*.

Mindfulness pertains to existing in a *relaxed state of attentiveness*, one that involves both the inner world of thoughts and feelings, as well as the outer world of actions and perceptions.

Choosing at least one activity each day, to carry out in a mindful manner (by giving it your full and undivided attention), helps considerably.

If you are chopping vegetables, take the time to absorb the colors, the textures, the smells, the motions, the tastes.

If you are exercising on a treadmill, take the time to feel your muscles moving as you walk, run, jog, speed up and slow down.

That having been said, one can learn to live the entirety of their day in *mindful* meditation.

There is no witness. There is no judgment. You have succeeded in becoming an observer without engaging the mind. Thoughts and feelings are simply thoughts and feelings; they are not who you are.

Before one can work toward transcending the mind, one must reprogram (reconfigure) the subconscious mind. This is what I had to do in order to eclipse a life filled with total negative media bombardment.

The battlefield of the mind is merely the war that plays out between dark (ego) and light (mindfulness), a battle that everyone must conquer.

Such is the journey towards self-realization, a journey in consciousness, a journey in metamorphosis, the quest for self-transformation, the journey of an observer, the journey to freedom. Such is the evolution of man.

How, then, does one get there?

Everywhere you turn, one can easily read articles and books about the power of the subconscious mind.

Like the hard drive on a computer that stores all pertinent computer files, so, too, is one's subconscious mind comparable to this particular analogy.

The subconscious is where one locates everything that is not located in one's conscious mind, such as previous life experiences and memories; these are our original files, so to speak.

In order to gain access to this databank of information, in order to make changes to the original files, one must bypass the conscious mind. This, then, allows one to neutralize the negatives of the past (because memories cannot be changed) in order to gain the positives in the now.

Meditation is but one avenue open to the seeker who wishes to upgrade their operating system.

At first, you will hear your own thoughts forming in your mind. You may quickly come to realize that there tends to be much continuous repetition to your thoughts. Herein lies the greatest challenge, for there will be many thoughts that will arise as you are attempting to meditate.

In the very beginning, you will find yourself getting lost in them. Trying to remain unattached to the chatter in your head is the most difficult part.

You merely wish to become an observer, standing at the sidelines, if you will. As soon as you pass judgment on what you are observing, the thoughts will drag you down.

Pretend that you are outside, observing the clouds as they float across the sky. Now imagine your thought forms as the very clouds that are passing you by.

It is in coming to this realization that you can honestly say *I have become a witness to my own mind.*

There may also be pictures and images that begin to filter through. Try to become a witness to these visualizations as well.

Do not engage with either the thoughts or the images. Simply accept them while remaining unattached. Do not judge them. Remember, you are merely the observer.

You may also notice your body responding (emotional reactions) to specific thought forms that are filtering through. Once again, you must step out of the emotion.

One should not allow an emotion to control them while in the physical body. You are merely the observer. You may continue to be the witness, but only without judgment.

Becoming a witness to thought forms, pictures, images and emotions, is not an easy task; however, it *is* something that needs to be practiced every day.

As you are able to experience success with this while in a meditative state, so, too, shall you be able to practice living a *waking meditation* throughout your entire day.

While it is imperative that you become aware of what goes on in your mind when you are going about your daily life, it is important that you continue to step back, thereby maintaining the stance of an objective observer.

When you are able to experience this with considerable success, you can say that you are practicing a mindfulness type of meditation.

It is also important to realize that there is a monumental difference between you (as the observer) and the things that are observed by you.

## You Are Everything ~ Everything Is You

As you become more of a witness to your own mind, your consciousness is becoming more aware of itself.

What this means is that the egoic mind will begin to become quiet so that you can learn to reside, in a pure and nonjudgmental way, in what can be called the real Self.

All of the varied forms of meditation have but one purpose: to introduce you to the experiencing of consciousness. With this, then, comes the realization that this is all there is.

As you dedicate yourself to this practice, on an intense and daily basis, you will begin to observe transformation on many levels, each as unique as the individual.

In addition to meditation, affirmations and visualizations can also be used as transformational tools, a way of bypassing the conscious mind.

Affirmations are personal statements written in both positive and present tense terms. The more emotion one evokes upon saying these affirmations aloud, the more powerful they become.

Affirmations are positive statements, or directions, you make to yourself in order to bring about changes in your subconscious behavior patterns to whatever you will them to be.

For affirmations to be effective, they must always be stated as positive, already accomplished, results.

*Wording them in futuristic terms*, such as [1] <u>I will be</u>, [2] <u>I am going to be</u>, or [3] <u>I would like to be</u> actually *prevents the changes from ever taking place* because we are always in the now.

Therefore, *giving energy to the positive trait*, such as <u>I am always Unselfishly Loving</u> *always supersedes the negative*, (as in <u>I will become Unselfishly Loving</u>).

You need to *feel*, *mean* and *believe* the words as you say them, or the affirmation will not be an effective tool.

When it comes to visualization, yet another medium, I find it incredibly difficult to see the pictures while also trying to put myself in the image.

It is quite difficult to get emotionally excited about a specific impression when all my mind sees are some dark and fuzzy attempts at a new reality.

Now that I have discovered Mind Movies,[78] an absolutely phenomenal metaphysical tool, I am able to visualize with increasing clarity. Mind Movies is a *multi-media tool* that allows you to create a vision of what you want, scored with your favorite song; the one that makes you feel good, the one that makes you want to dance, the one that makes you smile and sing along.

*Freedom experienced on an inner level* is the very freedom that all seek, for it is the *real freedom*; this is what you experience when you are able to still the mind.

A calm mind is a powerful mind.

Peace, contentment, happiness and bliss are to be found when one experiences this silence, this stillness, this sense of calm.

---

[78] http://www.mindmovies.com/?10107

Accordingly, there are also additional benefits.

You will find that your ability to concentrate improves.

You will find that you have more patience, showing more tact in responding to difficult situations.

You will find that others do not hold as much sway over you (what they think of you and say about you), as before.

You will find yourself responding to situations with less anxiety and worry.

As difficulties arise, you will demonstrate an increased ability to maintain a sense of inner poise and common sense.

You will find that you are sleeping better.

In addition, all of the above vastly improves your ability to meditate. Inner peace enables one to feel grounded, to feel balanced. In these stressful times, this is what is needed by all.

Developing the inner ability to still the mind (through such tools as meditation, detachment, visualizations, affirmations and yoga) will take you a considerable distance towards both attaining *and* maintaining inner balance and peace of mind.

Cultivating a "nonjudgmental awareness of the present bestows a host of benefits; mindfulness reduces stress, boosts immune functioning, reduces chronic pain, lowers blood pressure, and helps patients cope with cancer. By alleviating stress, spending a few minutes a day actively focusing on living in the moment reduces the risk of heart disease. Mindfulness may even slow the progression of HIV." [79] In addition, "mindful people are happier, more exuberant, more empathetic, and more secure. They have higher self-esteem and are more accepting of their own weaknesses. Anchoring awareness in the here and now reduces the kinds of impulsivity and reactivity that underlie depression, binge eating, and attention problems. Mindful people can hear negative feedback without feeling

---

[79] Dixit, Jay. (2008) *The Art of Now: Six Steps to Living in the Moment* article accessed on March 21, 2011 at http://www.psychologytoday.com/articles/200810/the-art-now-six-steps-living-in-the-moment

threatened. They fight less with their romantic partners and are more accommodating and less defensive. As a result, mindful couples have more satisfying relationships." [80]

As Ellen Langer, a psychologist at Harvard and author of <u>Mindfulness,</u> states …... *"When people are not in the moment, they're not there to know that they're not there. Overriding the distraction reflex and awakening to the present takes intentionality and practice."* [81]

Michael Kernis, a psychologist at the University of Georgia, says that *"when people are mindful, they're more likely to experience themselves as part of humanity, as part of a greater universe.* That's why highly mindful people such as Buddhist monks talk about being one with everything." [82]

---

[80] Dixit, Jay. (2008) *The Art of Now: Six Steps to Living in the Moment* article accessed on March 21, 2011 at http://www.psychologytoday.com/articles/200810/the-art-now-six-steps-living-in-the-moment
[81] Ibid.
[82] Dixit, Jay. (2008) *The Art of Now: Six Steps to Living in the Moment* article accessed on March 22, 2011 at http://www.psychologytoday.com/articles/200810/the-art-now-six-steps-living-in-the-moment?page=2

How many times have you completely entangled yourself, either by worrying about the future or reliving the past?

As long as you continue to engage in such thoughts, you are unable to joyfully experience the now.

It is imperative that you take the time to derive pleasure from whatever it is that you are doing in the present moment. Taking the time to savour the feelings, the smells, the tastes and sounds, will allow you to experience more joy, more happiness and more gratitude in your life.

As well you know, most negative thoughts involve either the past or the future. It was Mark Twain who wrote … *I have known a great many troubles, but most of them never happened.*

When you find yourself worrying about something that has not happened, and may not happen all, you become depressed and your anxiety increases.

In effect, worrying is a situation where you continue to torment yourself about the uncertainties of the future.

The moment you bring yourself into awareness of the present moment, you have been freed from worry.

Brooding about happenings of the past, situations whereby you are unable to let things be, also contributes to a troubled state. The moment you bring yourself into awareness of the present moment, you have been freed from unnecessary agitation.

It is of the utmost importance that you begin to develop and cultivate an awareness of how you interpret and react to what is happening in your life.

In becoming the ever mindful observer, you have the opportunity to acknowledge the emotion that is being felt. In stepping back to observe how you are feeling and responding, setting aside both anger and fear, you allow yourself additional time to counter the initial response(s) with mindfulness.

Through the art of inhabiting your own mind more fully, not only does this affect you in a more positive way; it also has a powerful effect on your interactions with others.

By "being open to the way things are in each moment without trying to manipulate or change the experience; without judging it, clinging to it, or pushing it away, the present moment can only be as it is. Trying to change it only frustrates and exhausts you. Acceptance relieves you of this needless extra suffering." [83]

Working with the neediest students, as a Special Education teacher, provides me with countless opportunities from which to keep learning this acceptance. As with life, there are certain things that are beyond your control; hence, you can only work within the confines of the situation while demonstrating nonjudgmental awareness. Suffice it to say that some days are easier for me than others.

While living a consistent mindful life takes time, diligence and effort, the mindfulness part is easy when you become focused on the present.

---

[83] Dixit, Jay. (2008) *The Art of Now: Six Steps to Living in the Moment* article accessed on March 22, 2011 at http://www.psychologytoday.com/articles/200810/the-art-now-six-steps-living-in-the-moment?page=4

"*Mindfulness is the only intentional, systematic activity that is not about trying to improve yourself or get anywhere else*," explains Kabat-Zinn. *It is simply a matter of realizing where you already are*. A cartoon from <u>The New Yorker</u> sums it up: Two monks are sitting side by side, meditating. The younger one is giving the older one a quizzical look, to which the older one responds: *Nothing happens next. This is it*." [84]

Taking the time to pay attention to your immediate experience, right here, right now, is what mindfulness is all about.

However, here is the most fundamental paradox of all.

Mindfulness "isn't a goal, because goals are about the future, but you do have *to set the intention of paying attention to what's happening at the present moment*. As you read the words printed on this page, as your eyes

---

[84] Dixit, Jay. (2008) *The Art of Now: Six Steps to Living in the Moment* article accessed on March 22, 2011 at http://www.psychologytoday.com/articles/200810/the-art-now-six-steps-living-in-the-moment?page=4

distinguish the black squiggles on white paper, as you feel gravity anchoring you to the planet, wake up. Become aware of being alive. And breathe. As you draw your next breath, focus on the rise of your abdomen on the in-breath, the stream of heat through your nostrils on the out-breath. If you're aware of that feeling right now, as you're reading this, you're living in the moment. Nothing happens next. It's not a destination. This is it. You're already there." [85]

---

[85] Dixit, Jay. (2008) *The Art of Now: Six Steps to Living in the Moment* article accessed on March 22, 2011 at http://www.psychologytoday.com/articles/200810/the-art-now-six-steps-living-in-the-moment?page=5

# Positive Living

In truth, there is no such thing as positive energy or negative energy. All energy is simply of a neutral intensity; that is, at least until we personalize it. It is through this process of personal differentiation that energy takes on either a positive or negative connotation (based on both personal beliefs as well as societal values).

We know there are emotions that make us feel good (happy, blissful, cheerful, elated, jubilant, overjoyed, thrilled, peaceful); hence, we refer to them as positive emotions.

We also know there are emotions that make us feel bad (agitated, upset, worried, troubled, exhausted, aloof, antagonistic); hence, we refer to them as negative emotions.

In addition, what is deemed positive, negative and/or neutral, is also based on the perception of the individual.

As most would attest, music is an incredibly powerful form of energy.

In fact, music is "the easiest way to shift your energy quickly. Athletes often listen to certain songs before games to help channel adrenaline; artists listen to music to help get their creative juices flowing; and many writers write with the help from music. While music is the easiest way to understand this concept, it is definitely not the only way to become energized." [86]

To fully engage in positive living, you need to acknowledge what it is that makes you feel happy, what it is that makes you feel whole, what it is that makes you feel peaceful, what it is that makes you feel ecstatic.

Make a list of everything that brings positive energy into your life. Some examples might include: spending time outdoors in the warm sunshine, smelling the air after a refreshing rain, listening to the waves as they break along the shore, listening to the sound of a waterfall, reading a book, listening to music, meditating, exploring new recipes, and focusing on gratitude, just to cite a few.

---

[86] Deitrick, Andrew. *Creating Positive Energy For Positive Change* article accessed on March 21, 2011 at http://tinybuddha.com/blog/on-creating-positive-energy-for-positive-change/

## You Are Everything ~ Everything Is You

When you learn to fully appreciate the moment, you begin to see that "you have profound power to manifest positive feelings within – to create divinely inspired energy, if you will, that impacts everything and everyone around you." [87] It is in this knowingness that all, eventually, come to realize their significance, their part, in the bigger picture.

You experience energies throughout your day. You also create energies on a daily basis. Some of these energies are powerful (easily recognizable), others are far more subtle; sometimes intuitively felt, sometimes not.

The things you say, the things you think, the actions you take, the actions you chose not to take – all of these create energy that impacts your life; so, too, does this energy impact the lives of the people around you.

If you are able to create more positive energy in your life, remaining upbeat in what may appear to be trying and challenging times, not only will you be witness to

---

[87] Deitrick, Andrew. *Creating Positive Energy For Positive Change* article accessed on March 21, 2011 at http://tinybuddha.com/blog/on-creating-positive-energy-for-positive-change/

improvements in your own life, but, so, too, will your feelings of joyfulness, hopefulness and contentment, your demonstrations of inner serenity and peace of mind, your affirmations of enthusiasm and exuberance for life, touch the lives of those around you.

Now is the time for all to "come to realize that despite our different beliefs, our different cultural norms, our different lifestyles, our different socioeconomic situations, we are all part of the same universe. Like a pebble thrown into a still pond, the ripples of negative energy eventually affect every corner of that pond, no matter how imperceptibly. We need to do our part, not to deny the existence of pebbles, but to make sure that as few as possible are thrown into the pond. None of us has all the answers, but we are all walking the path that seems right for us at this point in time. We must all be allowed that right *as long as exercising that right does not interfere with another's right to do the same.* We should be able to exercise that right with no fear of condemnation from others because their views differ from ours." [88]

We also need to recognize that "harming any one part of the universe harms all the parts. The good news here is that the opposite is also true. When one part is healed, all parts are better off for it. In the end, it comes down to our choice: are we going to use positive or negative energy to resolve a given situation." [89]

In every moment, you "have a choice: to be at peace or to be in resistance. When you are at peace, you attract positive energy, and when you resist, you create negative vibes that reflect back on your being. It's a simple choice and yet most people unconsciously choose to live in negativity." [90]

---

[88] *Negative and Positive Energy* article accessed on March 22, 2011 at http://rainbowsendpress.com/troe/negposenrgy.html
[89] Ibid.
[90] *How to Attract Positive Energy and Dispel Negative Energy* article accessed on March 22, 2011 at http://www.outofstress.com/attract-positive-energy/

Do you acknowledge the importance behind implementing what Yeshua (Jesus) called the Golden Rule to be important?

Do you recognize the importance of treating others the way you want to be treated?

Do you endorse the importance of starting each day in thoughtful and introspective silence (meditation), which generates positive energy, as compared to resentment, which merely generates more negativity?

Do you agree that there is positive to be found in every situation, knowing that good and bad are just perceptions that you have created in your own mind?

Do you support the visualization of a more peaceful life for yourself?

Do you accept your faults, knowing that you are willing to grow towards healing and strength as an individual?

Are you able to feel compassion towards yourself, knowing that you are doing the best that you can at any given time?

Do you listen to, and try to understand, the perspectives of others, regardless of how different they may be from your own?

Are you able to express your true self (in thoughts, actions, words and deeds), gently and honestly, while also allowing others, without condemnation, to do the same?

Do you celebrate the success and happiness of other people as opposed to allowing jealousy and cynicism to harden your heart?

It becomes in answering each of the aforementioned questions honestly, that you can begin to make the intentional (conscious) choices to dispel negative energies from your life.

Additional ways of generating more positive energy might include listening to uplifting music, reading an inspirational book, watching an inspirational movie, spending time around positive and uplifting people, as well as practicing positive affirmations.

People "with positive energy are determined to do their best, and to see the best in the world around them. People with positive energy don't focus on "should have" or idealized, perfect expectations that are impossible to live up to. People with positive energy have an open heart and a sense of humor. People with positive energy don't care about being popular or keeping up with the Jones's – and they stay in touch with their hearts and souls. They know what they want to create and manifest in their lives." [91]

Anger, "if it is recognized and acknowledged, can become positive energy to enable us to change the circumstances we are angry about." [92]

Anger, then, becomes a powerful tool, when expressed through feelings derived from the heart (as opposed to the solar plexus).

---

[91] Pawlik-Kienlen, Laurie. (2007) *How Positive Energy Can Change Your Life* article accessed on March 22, 2011 at http://www.suite101.com/content/its-no-secret-a14334

[92] http://www.lifepositive.com/Mind/Relationship/Anger_as_positive_energy22004.asp

Noetic Science refers to the study of human thought. Perfecting one's mind, via their consciousness, is what provides us with the emotional freedom that is needed.

Interestingly enough, the power of the human mind is what the ancient mysteries were all about.

In truth, the ancients understood thought more profoundly than we do today. With such knowledge, however, also comes great responsibility.

The basic premise of Noetic Science correlates with the untapped potential of the human mind.

Experiments have shown that human thought, if properly focused, has the ability to affect, and change, one's physical world on a significant level. Indeed, this is what one can refer to as *mind over matter*.

It is also what has been termed *cosmic consciousness*, meaning that a vast amalgamating of human intention is more than capable of interacting with physical matter. Such can be achieved by way of mass meditation and prayer.

Lynne McTaggart defines cosmic consciousness as being *an energy capable of changing the physical world*. This energy, while outside the confines of the physical body, is a highly ordered energy.

Focused thought can affect anything. Indeed, human intention, when utilized in this way, can affect the world.

Dr. Masaru Emoto, a creative and visionary Japanese researcher, spent many years studying water, all of which can be viewed in his book, <u>The Message From Water</u>.

The human body can range anywhere from 55% to 78% water, depending on physical size.

The blood in the body contains almost 70% water.

Over 70% of the surface of the planet is covered with water.

In reference to the findings of Dr. Emoto, all of these interrelated components become unequivocally important.

Dr. Emoto was able to provide factual evidence that *human vibrational energy* (in the form of thoughts and words) *is able to affect the molecular structure of water*.

With water being the source of all life, its quality and integrity were also noted as being extremely important components.

Dr. Emoto and his fellow colleagues were witness to the reaction of water in keeping with different environmental conditions, including pollution and music.

Their findings have stated that water is alive.

We can naturally structure water through the use of positive and loving emotions, meaning that water is highly responsive to thoughts and words.

The research of Dr. Emoto has provided us with physical evidence that we can *positively heal and transform this planet* by the thoughts that we choose to think and the actions we choose to take (in direct association with those thoughts). Such can also be said for ourselves.

The power of intention and prayer appears to influence the water. The higher the purity of the intent, the less of a difference was denoted, when distance was an operating variable.

That having been said, *the crystalline structure of the water appears to reflect the composite vibrations* (energy) *being received.*

It is becoming increasingly more clear that human thought can, quite literally, transform one's physical world.

This means that the mind, via the consciousness, has the ability to alter the state of matter. In addition, and perhaps even more importantly, the mind also has the power to encourage the physical world to move in a specific direction.

Does this not mean that we are masters of our own universe?

What, then, is it that turns possibility into reality?

Could it actually be said, then, that the most essential ingredient in creating our universe is the *consciousness* that observes it? What are we, if not the *consciousness* that observes?

As consciousness, we have incredible powers.

We can heal the world.

We can heal ourselves.

We can heal our communities.

We can make our world exactly as we wish it to be.

Harnessing the true power of the mind, like meditation, requires extensive practice.

For some time now, I have been saying that based on the way we think and feel, we make the choice to emit either negative vibrations or positive vibrations.

Taken one step further, this also means that the way I think and feel enables me to be able to change myself for the better (or not).

If a continued vibration of positive energies from a great multitude of persons were to exist on a daily basis, with clear and loving intent, the world would be affected on a global scale.

This is the very premise that exists behind Noetic Science.

In the words of Mahatma Ghandi …… *Keep your thoughts positive because your thoughts become your words. Keep your words positive because your words become your behaviors. Keep your behaviors positive because your behaviors become your habits. Keep your habits positive because your habits become your values. Keep your values positive because your values become your destiny.*

Knowing that God is in you and all around you, courtesy of the unified field, so, too, is God "intimately involved in every thought you think and every action you take. And, you are also intimately involved with every other person and thing on this planet. You are never alone. You cannot say you have no responsibility for the things happening in the world." [93]

In short, positive living can be equated to living in the moment.

Now that you know what this constitutes, it is essential that you take the time to embrace this concept on a daily basis.

---

[93] The Center For Unhindered Living website accessed on March 19, 2011 at http://www.unhinderedliving.com/connectedtoall.html

## You Are Everything ~ Everything Is You

As you are able to heal yourself, so, too, does the world, as a collective whole, experience healing.

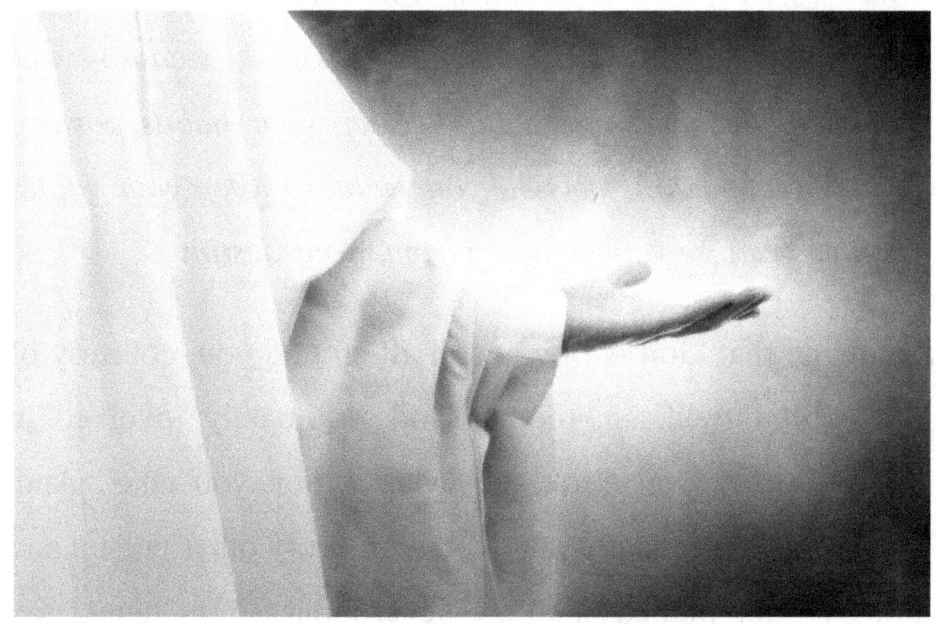

## Positive Energy Quotes

Life engenders life. Energy creates energy. It is by spending oneself, that one becomes rich.

Sarah Bernhardt

Energy is the power that drives every human being. It is not lost by exertion but maintained by it, for it is a faculty of the psyche.

Germaine Greer

The higher your energy level, the more efficient your body. The more efficient your body, the better you feel and the more you will use your talent to produce outstanding results.

Tony Robbins

The difference between **can** and **cannot** are only three letters; three letters that determine your life's direction.

Remez Sasson

When you wholeheartedly adopt a *with all your heart* attitude and go out with the positive principle, you can do incredible things.

Norman Vincent Peale

Work joyfully and peacefully, knowing that right thoughts and right efforts will inevitably bring about right results.

James Allen

The best is yet to be.

Robert Browning

The difference between an optimist and a pessimist is that an optimist thinks this is the best possible world. A pessimist fears that this is true.

Unknown Author

The moment of enlightenment is when a person's dreams of possibilities become images of probabilities.

Vic Braden

The nice part about being a pessimist is that you are constantly being either proven right or pleasantly surprised.

George Will

Throughout the centuries there were men who took first steps, down new roads, armed with nothing but their own vision.

Ayn Rand

Yesterday ended last night. Every day is a new beginning. Learn the skill of forgetting and move on.

Norman Vincent Peale

It's not the situation, but whether we react (negative) or respond (positive) to the situation that's important.

Zig Zigler

All you have to do is know where you're going. The answers will come to you of their own accord.

Earl Nightingale

Nurture your mind with great thoughts, for you will never go any higher than you think.

Benjamin Disraeli

## You Are Everything ~ Everything Is You

Remember, happiness doesn't depend upon who you are or what you have, it depends solely upon what you think.

Dale Carnegie

It is only with the heart that one can see rightly, what is essential is invisible to the eye.

Antoine Saint-Exupéry

## Life Force Energy

In Japan, they call it *ki*. The Chinese, referring to it as *chi*, have actually been able to map its movement throughout the physical body (courtesy of the meridians). Yoga adepts from India cite its name as *prana*. In the West, Dr. Wilhelm Reich, upon discovering the same energy, labeled it *orgone energy*. Russian researchers, in turn, have termed it *bio-plasmic energy*.

The knowledge that our bodies are filled with life force energy (referenced by any of the names denoted above) and that this life force energy is directly connected with our health ...... such has been part of a wisdom that has been in existence for thousands of years. As a result, there are many different forms of energy healing.

The amount of life force energy within your body varies from day to day, depending on a multitude of factors: the foods you eat, the liquids you drink, the air you breathe and the energy you absorb through your auric field, to cite just a few noteworthy elements.

This life force energy can be found everywhere. Given that it is the connective force of the universe, so, too, is there a limitless supply.

There are three main sources of life force energy, as paraphrased below. [94]

[1] Solar: required for approximately 20 minutes each day (either before 11:00 AM or after 3:00 PM), this invigorating form promotes good health (vitamin D).

[2] Air: absorbed into the lungs through breathing, this life force energy is absorbed by the energy centers of the body (chakras). Deep, slow, rhythmic breathing allows one to absorb more life force energy than short, shallow breaths.

[3] Ground: absorbed through the soles of the feet, meaning, of course, that walking barefoot increases the amount of life force energy absorbed by the body. Availing of more ground energy, in connecting with Mother Earth, increases your vitality levels, allowing you to think more clearly.

---

[94] http://www.healing-journeys-energy.com/Chi.html

When your life force energy is high, you feel healthy, fit, strong and full of stamina; you also feel confident, ready to take on the challenges that present themselves to you.

By comparison, when your life force energy is low (given the fact that there is either a restriction or a blockage in its flow), you feel weak, tired, listless and lethargic. This is when one is more vulnerable to illness and/or disease; especially if the energy depletion continues to last for a considerable period of time. It is important, therefore, to learn how to replenish your life force energy.

To understand healing from a Buddhist perspective, the mind is the creator of sickness and health. If mind (meaning both thought as well as consciousness) is the creator, as many of us believe, then the cause of disease is internal as opposed to external.

Buddhism asserts that "everything that happens to us now is the result of our previous actions, not only in this lifetime, but in other lifetimes. What we do now determines what will happen to us in the future," [95] meaning that in order to heal present (as well as future) sickness, we have to engage in positive actions now.

Buddhism also states that "for lasting healing to occur, it is necessary to heal not only the current disease with medicines and other forms of treatment, but also the cause of the disease, which originates from the mind. If we do not heal or purify the mind, the sickness and problems will recur again and again." [96]

Therefore, "by ridding the mind of all its accumulated garbage, all of the previously committed negative actions and thoughts, and their imprints, we can be free of problems and sickness permanently. We can achieve ultimate healing: a state of permanent health and happiness. In order to heal the mind and hence the body, we have to eliminate negative

---

[95] *Healing: A Tibetan Buddhist Perspective* article accessed on March 23, 2011 at http://www.buddhanet.net/tib_heal.htm
[96] Ibid.

thoughts and their imprints, and replace them with positive thoughts and imprints." [97]

Many have stated the basic root of our problems, which may also include sickness, to be selfishness (the inner enemy) in that selfishness "causes us to engage in negative actions, which place negative imprints in the mindstream. These negative actions can be of body, speech or mind, such as thoughts of jealousy, anger and greed. Selfish thoughts also increase pride, which results in feelings of jealousy towards those higher than us, superiority towards those lower than us, and competitiveness towards equals. These feelings in turn result in an unhappy mind, a mind that is without peace. On the other hand, thoughts and actions directed to the well-being of others bring happiness and peace to the mind." [98]

In continuation with this Buddhist belief, "the state of mind at the time of death is vitally important and can have a considerable effect on the situation into which we are reborn; hence, the need to prepare well for death and to be

---

[97] *Healing: A Tibetan Buddhist Perspective* article accessed on March 23, 2011 at http://www.buddhanet.net/tib_heal.htm
[98] Ibid.

able to approach our death with a peaceful, calm and controlled mind." [99]

Visualization can greatly assist with healing. One method (that I have utilized) is to visualize a ball of white light above my head, with the light spreading outward, completely enveloping me.

Take the time to imagine this light spreading throughout your body, completely dissolving all sickness, all problems, all negativity, totally concentrating (and affirming, with gratitude) on the image of your body, *already completely healed*.

So, too, have I used my crystals while visualizing the healing energy of the universe transforming my body into light.

The aim of practices such as these is to heal the mind as well as the body. In addition, one may also avail of meditation, yoga, imagery and progressive muscle relaxation.

---

[99] *Healing: A Tibetan Buddhist Perspective* article accessed on March 23, 2011 at http://www.buddhanet.net/tib_heal.htm

Another powerful method, in Buddhism, is "to meditate on the teachings known as thought transformation. These methods allow a person to see the problem or sickness as something positive rather than negative. *A problem is only a problem if we label it a problem.* If we look at a problem differently, we can see it as an opportunity to grow or to practice, and regard it as something positive. If someone gets angry at us, we can choose to be angry in return or to be thankful to them for giving us the chance to practice patience and purify this particular karma. It takes a lot of practice to master these methods, but it can be done." [100]

The compassionate mind is a calm, peaceful, joyful and stress-free environment; a mental environment that is ideal for healing.

In keeping, "by reaching out to others we become aware of not just our pain, but the pain ... of all beings." [101]

---

[100] *Healing: A Tibetan Buddhist Perspective* article accessed on March 23, 2011 at http://www.buddhanet.net/tib_heal.htm
[101] Ibid.

An iceberg is "a great analogy that describes the connection between the conscious and the subconscious mind: with a small, visible part above the surface and a huge part below. The conscious mind is responsible for our awareness in the waking state. Thinking analytically, creating logical order, wondering about cause and effect and asking "why" are all characteristics of the conscious mind. The conscious mind is the place of cognitive learning and understanding and uses the intellect to come up with logical solutions for problems. It makes choices based on facts and moves the body deliberately." [102]

In keeping with this iceberg analogy, "the subconscious mind is the vaster and more substantial part of our mind." [103]

One of the major tasks of the subconscious "is to help us define ourselves and make sense of the world. It uses emotions, memories, core values and beliefs as "filters" to sift through the otherwise overwhelming amount of

---

[102] *Accelerated Healing, Change and Self-Empowerment Through Mind-Body-Spirit Integration* article accessed on March 22, 2011 at http://www.cellularwisdom.com/body-mind-healing.shtml
[103] Ibid.

information we are exposed to and condense it to a size that is consciously comprehensible. In other words, whatever we perceive as "reality" is largely determined by our subconscious filter." [104]

The root causes of many emotional and physical problems reside in the subconscious mind.

For example, "unexpressed and unresolved memories and emotions that are stored within the subconscious mind can function as negative, limiting filters and lead to chronic anxiety, phobias, depression, addictions and low self-esteem. Limiting core beliefs, such as "I am not good enough" or "I am not safe" are imprinted on subconscious levels and can keep us stuck and prevent us from seeing who we really are and accessing our true potential." [105]

In continuation, "once the subconscious storage capacity is exhausted, negative emotions begin to accumulate in the

---

[104] *Accelerated Healing, Change and Self-Empowerment Through Mind-Body-Spirit Integration* article accessed on March 22, 2011 at http://www.cellularwisdom.com/body-mind-healing.shtml
[105] Ibid.

physical body, which can weaken our immune-system and lead to chronic pain, inflammation of the joints and auto-immune diseases. This transference of emotions, from the subconscious mind to the body may not only be about creating additional storage room, but also functions as a form of subconscious communication, letting us know, that it is time to address these unresolved emotional issues." [106]

In working consciously with the subconscious mind, "we can identify and address the deeper root causes of our challenges, remove and change subconscious filters and can effectively create profound and permanent changes on the mental, emotional and physical level." [107]

It was Norman Vincent Peale, a pastor at the Marble Collegiate Church in New York City, who wrote a wildly popular book, The Power of Positive Thinking, a book that

---

[106] *Accelerated Healing, Change and Self-Empowerment Through Mind-Body-Spirit Integration* article accessed on March 22, 2011 at http://www.cellularwisdom.com/body-mind-healing.shtml
[107] Ibid.

urged "ordinarily Americans to employ mind-body ideas to help themselves." [108]

It was Norman Cousins who wrote <u>The Anatomy of an Illness (as Perceived by the Patient)</u> in which he "told how he defeated his own severe physical ailment through laughter (including watching Marx Brothers movies)." [109]

Eastern medicine practices, like Chinese medicine and Ayurveda, have long embraced the concept of mind and body being interlinked, while we, here in the west, still prefer to treat both body and mind as separate units.

However, "several scientists and researchers are beginning to acknowledge the mind's role in healing and looking to leverage the effects of a positive state of mind in order to create better health." [110]

---

[108] *The Cure Within: Can the Mind heal the Body?* article accessed on March 22, 2011 at http://www.mindpowernews.com/CureWithin.htm
[109] Ibid.
[110] *Do Diseases Originate in the Mind? Can Emotions Heal the Body?* article accessed on March 22, 2011 at
http://www.suite101.com/content/do-diseases-originate-in-the-mind-can-emotions-heal-the-body-a323062

If a thought "has been thought repeatedly for a long time, it becomes a belief. Dr. Bruce Lipton, an internationally recognized cellular biologist and author of the book, <u>The Biology of Belief</u>, believes that, genes are actually manipulated by a person's belief system. It means that genes don't themselves cause a condition, except when they are triggered by the environment composed of one's thoughts, emotions and beliefs." [111]

Now *that* is an amazing statement; a statement that more than adequately sums up what I, too, have come to believe.

Dr. Christiane Northrup, author of <u>Women's Bodies, Women's Wisdom</u>, denotes that "emotions and thoughts are always accompanied by biochemical reactions" [112] in the body, meaning that the "cells in our bodies are memory banks that have imprints of events that the conscious mind might be unaware of. To create health, one must decide to

---

[111] *Do Diseases Originate in the Mind? Can Emotions Heal the Body?* article accessed on March 22, 2011 at http://www.suite101.com/content/do-diseases-originate-in-the-mind-can-emotions-heal-the-body-a323062
[112] Ibid.

be happy and make a conscious effort to uncover the programming of the body." [113]

This is yet another most insightful demonstrated scientific connection linking emotions, thoughts and mind to the state of one's health and well-being.

The medical field is finally beginning to acknowledge that the attitude of the patient has a very large impact on how fast that patient heals or even on whether he (she) survives a certain procedure.

A large number of medical studies are continuing to demonstrate that "negative emotions play a significant role in the development of heart diseases, chronic pain, autoimmune diseases and cancer. Anxiety, anger, shame and sadness drain our energy and suppress our immune system. Stress-related illnesses are the number one cause of death in the US. Self-sabotaging or addictive behaviors keep us stuck

---

[113] *Do Diseases Originate in the Mind? Can Emotions Heal the Body?* article accessed on March 22, 2011 at
http://www.suite101.com/content/do-diseases-originate-in-the-mind-can-emotions-heal-the-body-a323062

in old, destructive patterns. Non-supportive self-talk such as "I can't do this" or "I don't deserve this" prevent us from accessing our full potential and achieving our goals. On the other hand, positive thinking, a self-empowered attitude and optimistic beliefs, both stimulate and enhance the healing process." [114]

David R. Hamilton acquired an honors degree in biological and medicinal chemistry, and a Ph.D. in organic chemistry, before working as a scientist in the pharmaceutical industry for several years.

His research into the mind-body connection ultimately led him to leave that profession and become a motivational speaker.

The author of <u>How Your Mind Can Heal Your Body</u>, Dr. Hamilton talks about the close and powerful connection between the mind and body.

---

[114] *Accelerated Healing, Change and Self-Empowerment Through Mind-Body-Spirit Integration* article accessed on March 22, 2011 at http://www.cellularwisdom.com/body-mind-healing.shtml

The power of thought can affect you in profound ways, particularly in regards to its truly incredible effect on your health, as is explored in detail within the pages of this book.

Exploring the power of visualization, belief, and positive thinking, and their effects on the body, Dr. Hamilton presents a revolutionary quantum-field healing meditation (through which you can change yourself on an atomic level), showing you how you can use your imagination and thought processes to combat disease, pain, and illness.

As a result, it is possible for science and belief systems to merge in an effective manner for healing.

An £1.8 million study "has been launched by scientists at Glasgow University to find out what effect stress has on the genetic make-up of the human body and whether any changes are then inherited by offspring. The study, backed by a European Research Council grant, will focus on the role of telomeres, structures that act as a protective shield for chromosomes." [115]

It is known "that stress can damage telomeres, shortening their length and leading to an increased susceptibility to the diseases of ageing, such as cancers and heart problems. The research team is trying to find out if damaged telomeres passed on by parents to children could also shorten their lifespan." [116]

Professor Pat Monaghan, the research team leader, said "the passage of stress-induced changes in telomere length between generations had never been studied before but the impact of such an inherited problem could be far-reaching. *Erosion of the telomeres – how fast they shorten – has a bearing on how fast the individual will age in later life*, Monaghan said. *If you start* (life) *with a shorter telomere*

---

[115] Scotsman.com (March 27, 2011). *Stressed parents passing on damaging DNA to children* article accessed on March 27, 2011 at http://www.scotsman.com/news/Stressed-parents-passing-on-damaging.6741068.jp
[116] Ibid.

*length, you have got less to lose. More of the cells in your body would reach the critical point sooner.”* [117]

This five-year study "will be carried out on birds, looking at how living with unpredictable environmental changes, known to be very stressful, can accelerate ageing and reduce life expectancy. But the researchers said the findings will help to provide a picture of what is happening in humans. Monaghan, from the Institute of Biodiversity Animal Health and Comparative Medicine, said: *If you have ever thought that stress is killing you, you may well be right.*" [118]

Truly, this is something worth reflecting on.

---

[117] Scotsman.com (March 27, 2011). *Stressed parents passing on damaging DNA to children* article accessed on March 27, 2011 at http://www.scotsman.com/news/Stressed-parents-passing-on-damaging.6741068.jp
[118] Ibid.

## Notable Comparisons

The Silk Routes (collectively known as the Silk Road) were important paths for cultural and commercial exchange between traders, merchants, pilgrims, missionaries, soldiers, nomads and urban dwellers from Ancient China, Ancient India, Ancient Tibet, the Persian (Parthian) Empire and Mediterranean countries for close to 3,000 years.

Receiving its name from the lucrative Chinese silk trade, this was the major reason for turning the connection of trade routes into an extensive trans-continental network.

The Old Silk Road has many tales to share with us, one being <u>The Lost Sutras of Jesus</u>.

The Emperor, Taizong, "envisioned China as the civilizing center of the world. He granted foreigners the rights and privileges of Chinese citizens," [119] welcoming those with

---

[119] Riegert, Ray and Moore, Thomas; editors. (2003) *The Lost Sutras of Jesus: Unlocking the Ancient Wisdom of the Xian Monks* (page 7). Berkeley, CA: Seastone.

beliefs alien to the Tang Dynasty. As a result, Monks from across Asia "were soon teaching in Xian and Chinese pilgrims set out for India to collect Buddhist scriptures." [120]

In 635 AD (the seventh century), Aleben, a Nestorian bishop from Persia, along with his followers, journeyed 3,000 miles along the Old Silk Road, to the Chinese Imperial city Chang-an (today known as Xian).

The text he carried "told of a savior who would free humankind." [121] It was not long thereafter that the monks were busy "rendering their sacred texts into Chinese characters." [122]

As Persian Christians, "Aleben and his band believed Mary was the mother of Jesus the man, not the god. They were captivated by the historical Jesus and treated his teachings like those of a sage." [123] While the Jesus Sutras do not carry

---

[120] Riegert, Ray and Moore, Thomas; editors. (2003) *The Lost Sutras of Jesus: Unlocking the Ancient Wisdom of the Xian Monks* (page 7). Berkeley, CA: Seastone.
[121] Ibid.
[122] Ibid, page 8.
[123] Ibid, page 13.

canon status, they clearly merge Christian philosophy with both Buddhist and Taoist thought.

The original documents, theorized by historians to have been written in Syriac (a language that would have been closely related to the native tongue of Jesus), have never been found; instead, "only ancient scrolls containing the Chinese translations remain." [124]

The Jesus of the Gospels "teaches a life of peace, humility, paradox and egolessness. It's a short step [thereafter] to the Asian concepts of action through non-action and compassion through transcendence of the self. By taking Buddhist and Taoist teachings on yin and yang, the eternal law within things, and the search for an end to manic activity, and then combining them with the parables of Jesus, the Sutras create a more complex and deeply visionary form of Christianity." [125]

---

[124] Riegert, Ray and Moore, Thomas; editors. (2003) *The Lost Sutras of Jesus: Unlocking the Ancient Wisdom of the Xian Monks* (page 9). Berkeley, CA: Seastone.
[125] Ibid, page 124.

The Church of the East broke away from the West just in time, then, to avoid both "the magnificence and the curse of St. Augustine of Hippo, who took the basic notion of original sin and built it into the destructive force it was to become. In looking at the theology of the Church of the East, we can see what Christianity without St. Augustine might have been like." [126]

It was St. Augustine who saw "humanity as almost irredeemably wicked and perverse, rejecting any idea of some innate goodness. Augustine was opposed in his time by the first British theologian on record, a monk named Pelagius, who argued the opposite, that human nature was basically good but had been corrupted and misguided by human weakness. The theology of Augustine triumphed in the West, but it was a theology similar to Pelagius' that triumphed in China." [127]

---

[126] Palmer, Martin. *Original Nature Not Original Sin: Extract from The Jesus Sutras* article accessed on March 26, 2011 at http://www.goldenageproject.org.uk/968.php
[127] Ibid.

The term *original nature* or *innate nature* occurs in both Taoist and Buddhist thought, signifying "that all life is innately good but becomes corrupt or loses its way through the compromises of life and existence." [128]

In these Christian Sutras from China "is the shape or outline of a post-Augustinian theology that the West itself needs in order to become free from the burden of original sin and thus reconfigure or rediscover Christianity. Given that original sin was unknown as a central theme of Christian thought before the early fifth century, it is possible to agree with Pelagius that true Christianity holds a notion of original goodness. In a post Augustinian Christian world, this rediscovery, embodied in the actual books and thoughts of a major ancient Church, may well be a version of Christianity that can speak to spiritual seekers today." [129]

---

[128] Palmer, Martin. *Original Nature Not Original Sin: Extract from The Jesus Sutras* article accessed on March 26, 2011 at http://www.goldenageproject.org.uk/968.php
[129] Ibid.

Given that Buddhism was practiced throughout the Persian (Parthian) Empire, many living in Jerusalem, during the time of Jesus, would have had some familiarity with this religion.

In fact, "Buddhism was practiced throughout the Parthian empire during those years and even began its spread to China through missionaries from Parthia beginning only a mere century before Jesus' birth. The borders of the Parthian empire spread all the way to Roman-occupied Jerusalem from India, where Buddhism began." [130]

Healers were "not so uncommon in Buddhism, but in Jerusalem they were mostly unheard of. Anyone with such abilities would have been seen as a prophet of God by many Jews, regardless of the source of their healing powers; others would have seen him as a devil. Such was the way in which Jesus was received." [131]

---

[130] Madsen, Isaac T. (2008) *Comparison Between Jesus and Buddha* article accessed on March 23, 2011 at
http://www.helium.com/items/1079256-jesus-and-buddhahttpwwwheliumcomitems1079256-jesus-and-buddhaedit
[131] Ibid.

The 27 books of the New Testament constitute the fundamental holy scripture of Christianity.

Without the four Gospels according to Matthew, Mark, Luke and John, "Christianity is virtually null and void. Recent epoch-making discoveries of old Sanskrit manuscripts in Central Asia and Kashmir provide decisive proof that *the four Greek Gospels have been translated directly from the Sanskrit*. A careful comparison, word by word, sentence by sentence, shows that the Christian Gospels are Pirate-copies of the Buddhist Gospels (combined, of course, with words from the OT). God's word, therefore, is originally Buddha's word." [132]

Christian Lindtner, of Denmark, states that the best way to engage in a serious study of the four New Testament Gospels "is to start by counting the number of verses, the

---

[132] Lindtner, Christian. *Jesus Is Buddha* website accessed on March 23, 2011 at http://www.jesusisbuddha.com/

number of words, the number of syllables and the number of letters that the Greek text, of course, consists of." [133]

While this might appear an unreasonable place to begin, he shares that in doing so, "you will soon see that the unknown authors of the Gospels must have paid extreme attention to each word and syllable, to their number and to their numerical value, what the Greeks call psêphos." [134]

In keeping, the authors of the New Testament also "paid great attention to the size of syllables, words and sentences. The technical term for this phenomenon is gematria, from the Hebrew gymtry, which, again, is from the Greek geômetría (first attested in Herodotus)." [135]

---

[133] Lindtner, Christian. (2003) *The Christian Lindtner Theory (CLR) of the Buddhist Origins of the New Testament Gospels* article accessed on March 23, 2011 at http://www.jesusisbuddha.com/CLT.html
[134] Ibid.
[135] Ibid.

One could then say that the Gospels, "at least to some extent, report geometrical figures, rather than historical facts." [136]

The Christian Lindtner Theory (CLT) briefly states that the Gospels, "perhaps even the New Testament books as a whole, are a Pirate-copy of the Buddhist Gospels, or of the Buddha's Testament." [137]

In speaking of pirate copies, he means that the Gospels "not only imitate the sense of the Sanskrit originals" [138] but so, too, do the Gospels "also imitate the form and the numerical values found at various levels in the original." [139]

Lindtner believes the Q Gospel (on which Matthew, Mark and Luke are said to be have been based) was a combination of several Buddhist Sanskrit texts; namely, the Mûlasarvâstivâdavinaya [abbreviated as MSV] and the

---

[136] Lindtner, Christian. (2003) *The Christian Lindtner Theory (CLR) of the Buddhist Origins of the New Testament Gospels* article accessed on March 23, 2011 at http://www.jesusisbuddha.com/CLT.html
[137] Ibid.
[138] Ibid.
[139] Ibid.

Saddharmapundarîka [abbreviated as SDP], saying that scholars have "failed to identify Q simply because they did not consider reading MSV and SDP in the original Sanskrit," [140] meaning that any serious comparison between the life and teaching of Buddha and Jesus "must start out by carefully comparing the original Greek and the Sanskrit texts." [141]

Both Buddha and Jesus taught compassion, selflessness and intolerance.

As historical characters, both Jesus and Buddha are worth recognizing.

Might there be a possibility that a connection exists between the two?

---

[140] Lindtner, Christian. (2003) *The Christian Lindtner Theory (CLR) of the Buddhist Origins of the New Testament Gospels* article accessed on March 23, 2011 at http://www.jesusisbuddha.com/CLT.html

[141] Lindtner, Christian. (May 2003) Book Review article accessed on March 23, 2011 at http://www.jesusisbuddha.com/lebenundlehre.html

Interesting comparisons are denoted in the research conducted by Suzanne Olsson, author of <u>Jesus in Kashmir: The Lost Tomb</u>, especially when she states that "the word Sakya is believed by many scholars to derive from the name Isaac ... and is directly linked with Gautama Buddha's family name, which is Shakya, Sakymanu or Shakimuni," [142] meaning that if these Sakyas are descendants of Isaac, then so, too, was Gautama Buddha a descendant of Isaac.

Could it be, then, that Buddha may have had Jewish grandfathers in the same lineage as Jesus? I see this as being something that merits further investigation.

Is it possible that such an exploration might well demonstrate the oneness of *all* world religions, thereby connecting the bloodlines of *all* peoples?

---

[142] Olsson, Suzanne. (2005) *Jesus in Kashmir: The Lost Tomb* (page 31). Charleston, SC: Booksurge.

# Passion

Passion is defined as [1] *any powerful or compelling emotion or feeling,* [2] *a strong or extravagant enthusiasm or desire for something,* [3] *an outburst of strong emotion or feeling.*

We all have a passion.

When you love what you do, so completely and thoroughly, you are at one with your Higher Self, with your divine essence.

When you fall in love with an idea to the point whereby it has become your passion, the divine is expressing through you.

When you love what you do, so completely and thoroughly, you are creating for yourself.

The most truly amazing thing is that you are also creating for others because this burning desire, as felt by you, can only serve to benefit another.

Locating your passion, demonstrating persistence and the will to achieve, and taking action while refusing to give up: *these are the very attributes* that will allow you to achieve that which you desire.

Find what it is that you love. Find what it is that gives you joy. Find that which gives your life meaning.

You will know when you have found your passion, your bliss, your burning desire.

Do not settle for anything less.

# Know Thyself

*To know thyself*, as Socrates said, is but the beginning of enlightenment.

*Insight occurs when, and to the degree that, one knows oneself* ... are words as spoken by Andrew Schneider, creator of The Soul Journey. [143]

The best way to balance karma is by fulfilling your *dharma*. You are here to use your gifts and talents "in service to the purpose and plan of conscious evolution for yourself and the quantum field of all sentient life on Earth." [144]

Knowing that we have the potential to become both conscious and aware of the essence that lies buried within, the essence that we all share, we also have the ability to be able to access our own personal unconsciousness, that some refer to as the void, for therein lies true enlightenment.

---

[143] http://www.thesouljourney.com/?a_aid=195
[144] http://www.heartcom.org/2011QuantumShift.htm

Become who and what you truly are by *listening to the God within you*.

Become who and what you truly are by both knowing and accepting that *God speaks through feelings*, for they will be your guide to truth, directing you onward toward your individual path of enlightenment.

Compassion is who you are.

The keys to compassion lie in your ability to embrace *all* experiences as part of the one, without judgment.

This is the greatest challenge that all must face as they move towards greater states of personal mastery, which is the return to our truest form.

Demonstrating love through compassionate allowing means that you must love others enough to *allow* the range of their experience.

So, too, is compassion what you allow yourself to Become.

Each individual is the true creator and controller of the life that they have chosen to live. The purpose of life is to be part of it. The key is to live life *consciously*. Likewise, you are here to *live fully* and *with intent*.

## You Are Everything ~ Everything Is You

As you continue to expand in both your knowingness and your wisdom, so do you continue to expand the consciousness of all life, which is what God is.

To be *happy*, to be *joyful*, to be *filled with peace*; this is the way back to the kingdom within.

To *know* that God is not separate from you, to *know* that you and God are one and the same; this is the way back to the kingdom within.

You are here to *live lives of unlimited love*. You are here to *live lives of unlimited joy*. If you choose to have these conditions within your lives, then you must first *become* that which you want to experience more fully.

You are *not* your successes. You are *not* your failures. You are *not* your poverty. You are *not* your pain. You are *not* your joy. You are *not* your fear. These are merely elements of the physical experience that you are here to partake of so that you may come to *know yourself* in all ways.

This is what Yeshua (Jesus) meant when he said that while you live in this world, you are not of this world.

The path chosen by each individual is wholly unique to that person.

Each path is a valid one, all leading to the same destination, all leading to their truest nature as guided by compassion.

This is why it is of the utmost importance to feel the feelings, to engage the emotions, to think the thoughts; for they are what shall allow you to experience yourself in all ways.

The darkness is a most powerful catalyst. This is something that must be reconciled within each and every being.

There are many feelings and emotions that find their root in the dark, those that you have come to know as fear, rage, anger, hate, jealousy, depression, control, violation, incest, suspicion, denial, pain, judgment, illness, disease, death, greed, bitterness and retribution.

The darkness is as much a part of you as is the light.

There is, however, a way to avoid the power of this darkness, a power which lies in making choices that do not embrace the dark.

Allowing darkness to exist does not mean that such has become your choice.

Allowing darkness to exist does not mean that it has been condoned by you.

Allowing darkness to exist simply indicates that you have acknowledged the existence of this force, a force that actually serves to remind us of the exact opposite.

Every event in life serves as a catalyst that moves you into new experiences of yourself.

Allowing is what provides you with the opportunity to transcend the polarities of light and dark, a feat that you accomplish by embracing both as equal expressions of the same force from which you come.

Compassion is your birthright.

Compassion is your truest nature.

Compassion allows you to view from an equal standpoint.

There is no judgment.

In breaking the cycles of collective response, you become the higher choice.

Mastery of compassion means redefining what your world means to you.

It is *not* about forcing change upon the world around you.

You, and only you, choose *how* you respond.

As a being of compassion, you are offered the opportunity to *transcend polarity while still living within the polarity*. This is what enables you to move forward with life, a life filled with freedom, resolution and peace.

Compassion means living in trust.

Compassion means living with joy.

Living a new truth must first start with the individual. You must have the wisdom and the courage to embrace this new life, this new truth, as your reality.

This reality must then be lived in a world that may not always support that truth. This was the undertaking of the entire earthly mission of the one we have come to know as Yeshua (Jesus).

Life is a spiritual endeavor. You are asked to become that which you most desire in your life.

Become the peace that you seek.

Become the compassion that you desire.

Become the forgiveness that you seek.

Become the love that you desire.

Be *not afraid* to demonstrate your Becoming. The healing of this world will come about as a result of the healing of your thoughts, feelings and emotions.

Who among you is willing to live the truth of a higher response?

Who among you is willing to live the truth of what life has always had to offer?

By virtue of service to yourself and others, so, too, do you serve the Creator; it is in this way that you *Become* the greatest gift that you can offer.

Your ability to express forgiveness, allowing others the outcome of *their* own experiences, without changing the nature of who you truly are, is the highest level of mastery to which you can attain.

Therein lies the healing of all illusion, all separation, all duality.

As in the truly remarkable Japanese "kokoro" (heart and soul), this is exactly what must happen for all ...... a merger of heart and mind, so that all of us may continue, in the years ahead, to live as we have always been meant to live.

In the words of Dr. Richard G. Petty ... *We are all imbued with some splinter of God consciousness, that God is experiencing through us, that we have purpose and that our relationship should be one of partnership rather than domination or servility. We should live a life that allows the expression of this intelligence, because in that way we evolve, grow and achieve ultimate satisfaction and happiness. The brain is a filter rather than a creator of consciousness and it is possible to develop the brain so that more of this consciousness is able to manifest. This squares well with the recent data on neuroplasticity and the impact of meditation on the structure and function of the brain. These ideas are familiar to anyone who has studied Hindu, Buddhist or Taoist philosophy, or the writings of mystics and contemplatives who have described the universe as the* **body of God**. [145]

---

[145] Olsson, Suzanne. (2005) *Jesus in Kashmir: The Lost Tomb* (pages 23 and 24). Charleston, SC: Booksurge.

## Additional Pertinent Messages

Dr. Masaru Emoto is chief of the Hado Institute in Tokyo. Hado (pronounced hadou to rhyme with shadow) means both *wave* as well as *move*. From a scientific standpoint, Hado refers to the intrinsic vibrational pattern at the atomic level in all matter (the smallest unit of energy). Its basis is the energy of human consciousness.

Having spent over twenty years researching hado measuring and water crystal photographic technology, Dr. Emoto was witness to the fact that *water can turn positive* when it receives the pure vibration of human prayer, no matter how far away.

The energy formula of Albert Einstein, $E=MC^2$, really means that Energy = number of people and the square of people's consciousness.

## You Are Everything ~ Everything Is You

I would like to ask all people, not just those living in Japan, but all around the world, to please help us to find a way out the crisis of this planet!

The prayer procedure is as follows.

Day: March 31st, 2011 (Thursday)

Time: 12:00 noon in each time zone

Please say the following ……

*To the waters of the Fukushima Nuclear Plant, we are sorry to make you suffer. Please forgive us. We thank you and we love you.*

Please say it aloud or in your mind. Repeat it three times as you put your hands together in a prayer position. Please offer your sincerest prayer. Thank you very much from my heart.

With love and gratitude, Masaru Emoto [146]

---

[146] http://emotopeaceproject.blogspot.com/

Kryon is a loving angelic entity, as channeled by Lee Carroll. Since the word Kryon is not proprietary, in the last years there have been many others, in many cultures, who have come to use the name Kryon in many forms. However, Lee is not affiliated with any other Kryon channeling by any other person, school, or organization using the name Kryon.

Channeling a message of hope on March 15, 2011, in reference to Japan, it is *compassion that creates significant change* on the planet.

Kryon reminds us that spirit does not judge humanity. Humans are free to do whatever they choose, based on the consciousness that is developed by their own vibrations.

He also reminds us that nuclear energy is no longer needed as there are many other readily available alternatives.

Most unfortunately, quite often disaster must occur before humanity sees what has always been before them – the promise of something better.

The time is upon us to create the next step. [147]

Insightful entries from the blog belonging to Anne Thomas.

A Letter from Sendai (March 14, 2011) [148]

Signs of Hope in Sendai (March 15, 2011) [149]

A Spirit of Endurance in Japan (March 17, 2011) [150]

Deciding to Stay in Sendai (March 18, 2011) [151]

---

[147] http://www.facebook.com/notes/kryon-lee-carroll/kryons-channelling-regarding-the-disasters-in-japan/137055349697856

[148] http://www.odemagazine.com/blogs/readers_blog/24755/a_letter_from_sendai

[149] http://www.odemagazine.com/blogs/readers_blog/24784/signs_of_hope_in_sendai

[150] http://www.odemagazine.com/blogs/readers_blog/24805/a_spirit_of_endurance_in_japan

[151] http://www.odemagazine.com/blogs/readers_blog/24828/deciding_to_stay_in_sendai

Recovering in Sendai (March 19, 2011) [152]

Hope and Reconstruction in Sendai (March 20, 2011) [153]

Reassuring News from Sendai (March 20, 2011) [154]

How Everything Fits Together (March 21, 2011) [155]

A Japanese Perspective (March 22, 2011) [156]

Whatever Lies In Your Heart (March 23, 2011) [157]

---

[152] http://www.odemagazine.com/blogs/readers_blog/24875/recovering_in_sendai

[153] http://www.odemagazine.com/blogs/readers_blog/24878/hope_and_reconstruction_in_sendai

[154] http://www.odemagazine.com/blogs/readers_blog/24911/reassuring_news_from_sendai

[155] http://www.odemagazine.com/blogs/readers_blog/24949/how_everything_fits_together

[156] http://www.odemagazine.com/blogs/readers_blog/24950/a_japanese_perspective

[157] http://www.odemagazine.com/blogs/readers_blog/24951/whatever_lies_in_your_heart

## You Are Everything ~ Everything Is You

I Am Because You Are (March 24, 2011) [158]

Social Barriers Yield to Compassion (March 27, 2011) [159]

Alive, Knowing the Continuity of Life (March 28, 2011) [160]

Healing in Sendai (March 31, 2011) [161]

Dignity in the Face of Trauma (March 31, 2011) [162]

A Sense of Oneness in Sendai (April 2, 2011) [163]

---

[158] http://www.odemagazine.com/blogs/readers_blog/25234/i_am_because_you_are

[159] http://www.odemagazine.com/blogs/readers_blog/25235/social_barriers_yield_to_compassion

[160] http://www.odemagazine.com/blogs/readers_blog/25236/alive_knowing_the_continuity_of_life

[161] http://www.odemagazine.com/blogs/readers_blog/25237/healing_in_sendai

[162] http://www.odemagazine.com/blogs/readers_blog/25238/dignity_in_the_face_of_trauma

[163] http://www.odemagazine.com/blogs/readers_blog/25239/a_sense_of_oneness_in_sendai

Prevailing in Sendai (April 7, 2011) [164]

The Spirit of Gambatte in Sendai (April 11, 2011) [165]

How Words Create the World We Live In (April 14, 2011) [166]

Learning to Cope with the Unpredictable (April 14, 2011) [167]

Beauty Amid Destruction (April 15, 2011) [168]

---

[164] http://www.odemagazine.com/blogs/readers_blog/25241/prevailing_in_sendai

[165] http://www.odemagazine.com/blogs/readers_blog/25242/the_spirit_of_gambatte_in_sendai

[166] http://www.odemagazine.com/blogs/readers_blog/25240/how_words_create_the_world_we_live_in

[167] http://www.odemagazine.com/blogs/readers_blog/25324/learning_to_cope_with_the_unpredictable

[168] http://www.odemagazine.com/blogs/readers_blog/25338/beauty_amid_destruction

## You Are Everything ~ Everything Is You

## Rebuilding Life in Sendai (May 25, 2011) [169]

---

[169] http://www.odemagazine.com/blogs/readers_blog/29574/rebuilding_life_in_sendai

# Conclusion

During the course of this writing, the world was also focused on Libya. Riots took place in Benghazi (February 15, 2011); the trigger being the mass protest over the arrest of a human rights activist. Two days later, a demonstration against the government resulted in the deaths of six demonstrators.

Five days into the uprising (February 20, 2011), the Libyan people were warned by Seif al-Islam el-Qaddafi, son of Colonel Muammar el-Qaddafi, that continued protests would cause their country to fall into civil war; a situation that would result in the breakup of the country, thereby inviting a Western takeover.

According to a tally by the group Human Rights Watch, Qaddafi's security forces had, up to that date, killed at least 173 people. However, witnesses and rights activist individuals were saying that there were more than 200 people dead and hundreds wounded.

Benghazi, the traditional hub of the country's eastern province, has long been a center of opposition to the Qaddafi government. On the morning of February 20, 2011, the residents of Benghazi were describing an ongoing battle for control of the city (with a population of about 700,000).

Thousands of protesters had occupied a central square in front of the courthouse, chanting, as they had been for several days, wanting to bring down the Qaddafi regime. Several protestors, on their way to a funeral procession, were gunned down. By afternoon, the protest had become a revolt.

A United Nations resolution was signed on March 17, 2011; one that authorized the imposition of a no-fly zone above Libya, the expansion of existing sanctions and a call for a ceasefire. It also endorsed the use of force (through short of occupation of the country) to protect Libyan civilians.

David Cameron (British Prime Minister), Nicolas Sarkozy (French President), Hillary Clinton (US Secretary of State) and 20 other world leaders met at the Elysee Palace (in Paris) on March 19, 2011.

Qaddafi's insistence on breaking the ceasefire (the sight of his tanks rolling into Benghazi) is what led to a determined and united response from world leaders; meaning that their hands were forced: there was no option other than military action.

Losing no time in launching their assault on the dictator's regime, their resolve was such that military action was launched within a couple of hours of having emerged from an emergency summit in Paris, with British, French and American forces beginning a massive bombardment of Libya's military infrastructure at about 4:45 pm on March 19, 2011.

While it is most difficult to know what to believe, given the disinformation that exists, it is imperative that one continue to use discernment. You will find several links listed under Voltaire Network at the end of the book.

There have been reports citing the use of radioactive depleted uranium weapons in Libya. As a reader, you can conduct your own research into this most problematic, humanitarian (invisible genocide) issue; hence, it is for our planetary brothers and sisters, in Libya, that I also dedicate this tome.

When things like this happen, one's spiritual practice becomes even more important.

There is a way to practice healthier, more adaptive, ways of relating to the horrendous news that all are exposed to every day, as has been suggested by Terry Patten.

It is important, first and foremost, to recognize that "there is no going back in time to a non-connected age. Our world is evolving into an interconnected planetary entity, and we are called to be planetary citizens. We are called to identify with, care for, and feel a real (not just abstract) sense of connection with all of our brothers and sisters in the human family." [170]

It is completely appropriate, then, to "offer sympathy, to donate, even to engage in direct assistance, if you feel so

---

[170] Email received from Terry Patten (http://www.integralspiritualpractice.com/) entitled *Technique Three – Practicing With Traumatic Events In The News* on March 19, 2011.

called, when disaster strikes in some part of the world. We're all in this journey of life together, and we all must rely on each other as a world community to face life's challenges and continue evolving together." [171]

By the same token, "it does little good for us to be chronically distracted by the 24/7, often over-dramatized news cycles, or neglecting the ways in which we could be growing stronger, individually or as a local community," [172] because we so focused on the problems of others.

Instead, Terry suggests the following.

*Occasionally, as a practice, devote a few minutes to <u>completely feeling</u> the news of the world. Once you know a little about what's going on, because you've seen the footage or read the stories of the terror and courage and heartbreak and heroism, take the time to <u>unplug</u> from every media source and shift your focus internally.*

---

[171] Email received from Terry Patten (http://www.integralspiritualpractice.com/) entitled *Technique Three – Practicing With Traumatic Events In The News* on March 19, 2011.
[172] Ibid.

## You Are Everything ~ Everything Is You

*Close your eyes and bring your attention to your body. Feel the tragic event in your head, your heart, your gut, your bones, your hands and feet, and then return to the center of your heart.*

*Feel the whole chaotic mix of feelings: the fear, the care, the despair, the strength, the acceptance, the raw humanity. Let your whole being simply witness it all, letting it flow through you.*

*Feel the space itself in which those feelings are arising. Feel your own awareness, and from there, simply observe what has happened and what it means. When you've relaxed into that spacious perspective, ask yourself, ask your heart: Is there anything I am specifically called to do?*

*Maybe that means making a donation to a relief organization.*

*Or it could mean taking an action to become better prepared locally in the event of a similar occurrence in your own community.*

*Or it could mean consciously learning more, or connecting with, and offering emotional support to, someone you know in the area.*

*On certain occasions it might even mean making a very serious life commitment to make a difference.*

*Or, it could also (and might often) simply mean feeling and offering your heartfelt compassion, silently "sending" your strength, light, clarity, and love to those affected.*

*Do whatever feels appropriate, and then let it go. Move on with your day, focusing on your moment-to-moment practice and life - with full and radiant gratitude for the mystery of existence and the gift of life we're blessed to be given.*

In the words of Sir Frances Bacon ... *This is a test to see if your mission on Earth is over. If you are still alive, it's not.*

Clearly, we still have much to learn.

# Bibliography

Babcock, Jon (translator). (2003) *The Lost Sutras of Jesus: Unlocking the Ancient Wisdom of the Xian Monks*

Braden, Gregg. (1995) *Awakening to Zero Point: The Collective Initiation*

Braden, Gregg. (1997) *Walking Between the Worlds: The Science of Compassion*

Braden, Gregg. (2000) *The Isaiah Effect: Decoding the Lost Science of Prayer and Prophecy*

Braden, Gregg. (2000) *Beyond Zero Point: The Journey to Compassion*

Braden, Gregg. (2004) *The God Code: The Secret of Our Past, The Promise of Our Future*

Braden, Gregg. (2004) *The Divine Name: Sounds of the God Code* (Audio Book)

Braden, Gregg. (2005) *The Lost Mode of Prayer* (Audio CD)

Braden, Gregg. (2005) *Unleashing The Power of The God Code: The Mystery and Meaning of the Message in Our Cells* (Audio CD)

Braden, Gregg. (2005) *An Ancient Magical Prayer: Insights from the Dead Sea Scrolls* (Audio Book)

Braden, Gregg. (2005) *Speaking the Lost Language of God: Awakening the Forgotten Wisdom of Prayer, Prophecy and the Dead Sea Scrolls* (Audio Book)

Braden, Gregg. (2005) *Awakening the Power of A Modern God: Unlock the Mystery and Healing of Your Spiritual DNA* (Audio Book)

Braden, Gregg. (2006) *Secrets of The Lost Mode of Prayer*

Braden, Gregg. (2007) *The Divine Matrix: Bridging Time, Space, Miracles and Belief*

Bunick, Nick. (2010) *Time for Truth: A New Beginning*

Chopra, Deepak. (1998) *The Path to Love: Spiritual Strategies for Healing*

Chopra, Deepak. (2005) *Peace Is The Way: Bringing War and Violence to An End*

Coelho, Paulo. (1998) *The Alchemist*

Coelho, Paulo. (2003) *Warrior Of The Light*

Das, Lama Surys. (1998) *Awakening the Buddha Within*

Das, Lama Surys. (2000) *Awakening to the Sacred: Creating a Spiritual Life From Scratch*

Das, Lama Surys. (2001) *Awakening the Buddhist Heart: Integrating Love, Meaning and Connection into Every Part of Your Life*

Das, Lama Surys. (2003) *Living Kindness: The Buddha's Ten Guiding Principles for a Blessed Life*

Das, Lama Surys. (2003) *Letting Go of the Person You Used To Be: Lessons on Change, Loss and Spiritual Transformation*

Doucette, Michele. (2010) *A Travel in Time to Grand Pré* (second edition)

Doucette, Michele. (2010) *The Ultimate Enlightenment For 2012: All We Need Is Ourselves*

Doucette, Michele. (2010) *Turn Off The TV: Turn On Your Mind*

Doucette, Michele. (2010) *Veracity At Its Best*

Doucette, Michele. (2011) *Sleepers Awaken: The Time Is Now To Consciously Create Your Own Reality*

Doucette, Michele. (2011) *Healing the Planet and Ourselves: How To Raise Your Vibration*

Gawain, Shakti. (1993) *Living In The Light: A Guide to Personal and Planetary Transformation*

Gawain, Shakti. (1999) *The Four Levels of Healing*

Gawain, Shakti. (2000) *The Path of Transformation: How Healing Ourselves Can Change The World*

Gawain, Shakti. (2003) *Reflections in The Light: Daily Thoughts and Affirmations*

Hansard, Christopher. (2003) *The Tibetan Art of Positive Thinking*

Hicks, Esther and Hicks, Jerry. (2004) *Ask and It Is Given: Learning to Manifest Your Desires*

Hicks, Esther and Hicks, Jerry. (2004) *The Teachings of Abraham: Well-Being Cards*

Hicks, Esther and Hicks, Jerry. (2005) *The Amazing Power of Deliberate Intent: Living the Art of Allowing*

Hicks, Esther and Hicks, Jerry. (2006) *The Law of Attraction: The Basics of the Teachings of Abraham*

Hicks, Esther and Hicks, Jerry. (2008) *The Astonishing Power of Emotions: Let Your Feelings Be Your Guide*

Hicks, Esther and Hicks, Jerry. (2009) *The Vortex: Where The Law of Attraction Assembles all Cooperative Relationships*

Koven, Jean-Claude. (2004) *Going Deeper: How To Make Sense of Your Life When Your Life Makes No Sense*

Kribbe, Pamela. (2008) *The Jeshua Channelings: Christ Consciousness in a New Era*

Lama, Dalai. (2004) *The Wisdom of Forgiveness: Intimate Conversations and Journey*

McTaggart, Lynne. (2003) *The Field: The Quest For The Secret Force Of The Universe*

McTaggart, Lynne. (2008) *The Intention Experiment: Using Your Thoughts to Change Your Life and the World*

Millman, Dan. (2000) *Way of the Peaceful Warrior*

Millman, Dan. (1991) *Sacred Journey of the Peaceful Warrior*

Millman, Dan. (1992) *No ordinary Moments: A Peaceful Warrior's Guide to Daily Life*

Millman, Dan. (1995) *The Life You Were Born To Live*

Millman, Dan. (1999) *Everyday Enlightenment*

Nichols, L. Joseph. (2000) *The Soul As Healer: Lessons in Affirmation, Visualization and Inner Power*

Olsson, Suzanne. (2005) *Jesus in Kashmir: The Lost Tomb*

Rasha. (1998) *The Calling*

Rasha. (2003) *Oneness*

*Kybalion* (a study of Hermetic philosophy pertaining to both ancient Egypt and ancient Greece)

Ruiz, Don Miguel. (1997) *The Four Agreements: A Practical Guide to Personal Freedom*

Ruiz, Don Miguel. (1999) *The Mastery of Love: A Practical Guide to The Art of Relationship*

Ruiz, Don Miguel. (2000) *The Four Agreements Companion Book*

Ruiz, Don Miguel. (2004) *The Voice of Knowledge: A Practical Guide to Inner Peace*

Ruiz, Don Miguel. (2009) *Fifth Agreement: A Practical Guide to Self-Mastery*

Sky, Michael. (2002) *The Power of Emotion: Using Your Emotional Energy to Transform Your Life*

Tolle, Eckhart. (1999) *The Power of Now: A Guide to Spiritual Enlightenment*

Tolle, Eckhart. (2001) *Practicing the Power of Now: Meditations, Exercises and Core Teachings for Living the Liberated Life*

Tolle, Eckhart. (2001) *The Realization of Being: A Guide to Experiencing Your True Identity* (Audio CD)

Tolle, Eckhart. (2003) *Stillness Speaks*

Tolle, Eckhart. (2003) *Entering The Now* (Audio CD)

Tolle, Eckhart. (2005) *A New Earth: Awakening to Your Life's Purpose*

Twyman, James. (1998) *Emissary of Peace: A Vision of Light*

Twyman, James. (2000) *The Secret of the Beloved Disciple*

Twyman, James. (2000) *Portrait of the Master*

Twyman, James. (2000) *Praying Peace: In Conversation with Gregg Braden and Doreen Virtue*

Twyman, James. (2003) *The Proposing Tree*

Twyman, James. (2008) *The Moses Code: The Most Powerful Manifestation Tool in the History of the World*

Twyman, James. (2009) *The Kabbalah Code: A True Adventure*

Twyman, James. (2009) *The Proof: A 40-Day Program for Embodying Oneness*

Zukav, Gary. (1998) *The Seat of The Soul*

Zukav, Gary. (2001) *Thoughts from The Seat of The Soul: Meditations for Souls in Process*

Zukav, Gary and Francis, Linda. (2001) *The Heart of The Soul: Emotional Awareness*

Zukav, Gary and Francis, Linda. (2003) *The Mind of The Soul: Responsible Choice*

Zukav, Gary and Francis, Linda. (2003) *Self-Empowerment Journal: A Companion to The Mind of The Soul: Responsible Choice*

Zukav, Gary. (2010) *Spiritual Partnership: The Journey to Authentic Power*

Wilcock, David. *The Shift of the Ages – Convergence Volume One* (online book) [173]

Wilcock, David. *The Science of Oneness – Convergence Volume Two* (online book) [174]

Wilcock, David. *The Divine Cosmos – Convergence Volume Three* (online book) [175]

Wilcock, David. *Wanderer Awakening: The Life Story of David Wilcock* (online book) [176]

---

[173] http://divinecosmos.com/start-here/books-free-online/18-the-shift-of-the-ages
[174] http://divinecosmos.com/start-here/books-free-online/19-the-science-of-oneness
[175] http://divinecosmos.com/start-here/books-free-online/20-the-divine-cosmos
[176] http://divinecosmos.com/start-here/books-free-online/25-wander-awakening-the-life-story-of-david-wilcock

## You Are Everything ~ Everything Is You

Wilcock, David. *The Reincarnation of Edgar Cayce* (online book) [177]

Wilcock, David. *The End of Our Century* (online book edited by David Wilcock) [178]

If you have the stomach for viewing photos of DU's impact on children, feel free to conduct a Google search. You can also visit Depleted Uranium (DU): Silent Genocide. [179] You are herein warned that the subject is very, very disturbing.

---

[177] http://divinecosmos.com/start-here/books-free-online/22-the-reincarnation-of-edgar-cayce-draft-of-pt-1
[178] http://divinecosmos.com/start-here/books-free-online/26-the-end-of-our-century
[179] http://www.mindfully.org/Nucs/2004/DU-Silent-Genocide25mar04.htm

# Websites

**2012**

2012, Galactic Cosmology and A New World Age [180]

2012: What's Really Happening – Space Weather, Mayan Prophecy and The True Meaning of The Apocalypse [181]

Interview with Carlos Barrios [182]

Shift of The Ages [183]

**Affirmations**

Affirmations for Health, Wellness and Healing [184]

---

[180] http://www.susanrennison.com/2012_Galactic_Cosmology_A_New_World_Age.pdf

[181] http://www.susanrennison.com/2012WhatsReallyHappening_jul20101.pdf

[182] http://www.earthchangesmedia.com/audioarchives.php

[183] http://www.shiftoftheages.com/

[184] http://www.suite101.com/content/affirmations-for-health-wellness-and-healing-a173512

Daily Positive Affirmation [185]

How and Why To Use Positive Affirmations as a Stress Management Tool [186]

Use Affirmations for Positive Changes in Life [187]

Vital Affirmations [188]

**Body, Mind, Spirit**

Body, Mind, Spirit Magazine [189]

Solve Your Problem: Body, Mind, Spirit Index [190]

---

[185] http://www.holistic-mindbody-healing.com/daily-positive-affirmation.html
[186] http://stress.about.com/od/optimismspirituality/a/positiveaffirms.htm
[187] http://www.suite101.com/content/affirmations-a-self-improvement-tool-part-2-a117385
[188] http://www.vitalaffirmations.com/
[189] http://www.saskworld.com/
[190] http://www.solveyourproblem.com/mind-body-spirit/index.shtml

## Buddhism

A Basic Buddhism Guide: The Eight Fold Path [191]

About Dharma [192]

A View on Buddhism [193]

Buddha's Noble Eight Fold Path and the Paradox of our Time [194]

Buddha Sasana [195]

Buddhism and Christianity [196]

Buddhist Electronic Books (free download) [197]

---

[191] http://www.buddhanet.net/e-learning/8foldpath.htm
[192] http://aboutdharma.org/index.php/
[193] http://viewonbuddhism.org/
[194] http://www.intentblog.com/archives/2006/08/buddhas_noble_e.html
[195] http://www.buddhanet.net/budsas/ebud/ebidx.htm
[196] http://www.buddhist-tourism.com/buddhism/religion/buddhism-christianity.html
[197] http://www.buddhanet.net/ebooks_m.htm

# You Are Everything ~ Everything Is You

Dharma Centre of Canada [198]

Dharma: The Path of Righteousness [199]

The Buddha's Noble Eight Fold Path [200]

The Buddha's Noble Eight Fold Path (online audio book) [201]

The Buddha's Noble Eight Fold Path [202]

The Eight Fold Path – Buddhist Path to Enlightenment [203]

The Noble Eight Fold Path [204]

The Noble Eight Fold Path [205]

---

[198] http://dharmacentre.org/
[199] http://hinduism.about.com/od/basics/a/dharma.htm
[200] http://www.sangharakshita.org/_books/Noble_Eightfold_Path.pdf
[201] http://www.naxosaudiobooks.com/541612.htm
[202] http://www.naturalawareness.net/8foldpath.pdf
[203] http://buddhism.about.com/od/theeightfoldpath/a/eightfoldpath.htm
[204] http://www.thebigview.com/buddhism/eightfoldpath.html
[205] http://www.accesstoinsight.org/lib/authors/bodhi/waytoend.html

The Wheel of Dharma and the Noble Eight Fold Path [206]

## Christian Lindtner Theory

Christian Lindtner Theory (CLT) of the Buddhist Origins of the NT Gospels [207]

Some Sanskritisms in the New Testament Gospels [208]

The Pope in the Footsteps of the Buddha [209]

## Consciousness

A Course in Consciousness [210]

Center for Consciousness Studies [211]

Global Consciousness Project [212]

---

[206] http://www.success360.com/coach/cultures_buddhism_dharma_n8p.html
[207] http://www.jesusisbuddha.com/CLT.html
[208] http://www.jesusisbuddha.com/somesan.html
[209] http://www.jesusisbuddha.com/pope.html
[210] http://faculty.virginia.edu/consciousness/
[211] http://consciousness.arizona.edu/
[212] http://noosphere.princeton.edu/

Journal of Consciousness Studies [213]

Meditations: Thoughts for the Scholars of Consciousness [214]

Quantum Consciousness [215]

**Cosmos**

Cosmological History of the Universe [216]

Divine Cosmos (David Wilcock) [217]

Magnetic Energy to Heal the Planet [218]

Order, Energy and God [219]

One Mind: One Energy [220]

---

[213] http://www.imprint.co.uk/jcs/
[214] http://www.jaredbhobbs.com/
[215] http://www.quantumconsciousness.org/publications.html
[216] http://www.thebigview.com/spacetime/universe.html
[217] http://divinecosmos.com/
[218] http://www.magneticenergy.org.uk/index.htm
[219] http://reality.lciweb.com/
[220] http://www.one-mind-one-energy.com/

The Big View Document Library Download [221]

The Proof (online course) [222]

The Words of Oneness through Rasha [223]

Truth Reality [224]

**Cyclic Universe Theory**

Cosmic Evolution in a Cyclic Universe [225]

The Cyclic Theory of the Universe (Paul J. Steinhardt) [226]

**Feng Shui**

Feng Shui Theory and Feng Shui Tools [227]

World of Feng Shui [228]

---

[221] http://www.thebigview.com/about/download.html
[222] http://promos.hayhouse.com/twyman/theproof/index.php
[223] http://www.onenesswebsite.com/
[224] http://www.spaceandmotion.com/
[225] http://www.physics.princeton.edu/~steinh/cyclic2.pdf
[226] http://www.physics.princeton.edu/~steinh/vaasrev.pdf
[227] http://fengshui.about.com/od/thebasics/qt/fengshui.htm
[228] http://www.wofs.com/

## Genealogy

Ancestry of Siddhärtha Gautama (Buddha) [229]

Genealogy of Bahá'u'lláh [230]

The Mahavamsa: Genealogy of Kings [231]

## Meditation

100 Benefits of Meditation [232]

Insight Meditation Online (free downloads) [233]

Meditation [234]

Meditation Manual [235]

---

[229] http://trees.ancestry.ca/tree/19956804/person/874758440
[230] http://www.bupc.org/genealogy/genealogy-of-bahaullah.pdf
[231] http://www.buddhanet.net/budsas/ebud/mahavamsa/gene.html
[232] http://www.ineedmotivation.com/blog/2008/05/100-benefits-of-meditation/
[233] http://www.buddhanet.net/xmedfile.htm
[234] http://www.healthandyoga.com/html/meditation.html
[235] http://users.erols.com/peterbb/meditman.htm

Psychology Today: The Science of Meditation [236]

Why Meditate? [237]

**Metaphysics**

35 Free Classic Self Improvement Books [238]

Free Mind Power Books [239]

Metaphysics and God [240]

Thomas Troward [241]

**Mind Power**

Brainwave Frequencies and Mind Powers [242]

---

[236] http://www.psychologytoday.com/articles/200105/the-science-meditation
[237] http://www.holistic-mindbody-healing.com/why-meditate.html
[238] http://affirmyourlife.blogspot.com/2009/09/35-free-classic-self-improvement-e.html
[239] http://freemindpowerbooks.com/
[240] http://www.whatismetaphysics.com/metaphysics-and-God.html
[241] http://divinewaves.com/troward/lawAndTheWord/law-and-the-word.html
[242] http://www.holistic-mindbody-healing.com/brain-wave-frequency.html

## You Are Everything ~ Everything Is You

How to Heal your Body Using your Mind [243]

Limiting Beliefs about Health [244]

Mind Powers: Levels of Consciousness [245]

Negative Thinking Patterns and Wellness [246]

Silva Mind Body Healing System [247]

Solve Your Problem: Empowerment Index [248]

Subconscious Mind Healing [249]

The Conscious Mind [250]

The Nocebo and Placebo Effects [251]

---

[243] http://www.mindalign.net/
[244] http://www.holistic-mindbody-healing.com/limiting-beliefs.html
[245] http://www.holistic-mindbody-healing.com/mind-powers.html
[246] http://www.holistic-mindbody-healing.com/negative-thinking-patterns.html
[247] http://www.silvamindbodyhealing.com/products
[248] http://www.solveyourproblem.com/empowerment/index.shtml
[249] http://www.holistic-mindbody-healing.com/mind-healing.html
[250] http://www.holistic-mindbody-healing.com/the-conscious-mind.html
[251] http://www.holistic-mindbody-healing.com/nocebo.html

The Power of Subconscious Mind [252]

The Science of Mind (Ernest Holmes) [253]

The Superconscious Mind [254]

TIME Magazine: How Your Mind Can Heal Your Body [255]

Unstress Your Life, Inspire Your Mind, Unleash Your Dreams [256]

Using the Mind to Heal the Body [257]

**Positivity**

A Positive Mental Attitude [258]

---

[252] http://www.holistic-mindbody-healing.com/power-of-subconscious-mind.html
[253] http://www.sacred-texts.com/eso/som/index.htm
[254] http://www.holistic-mindbody-healing.com/superconscious.html
[255] http://www.time.com/time/covers/1101030120/
[256] http://ianpaulmarshall.com/
[257] http://appliedsportpsych.org/resource-center/injury-&-rehabilitation/articles/imagery
[258] http://www.holistic-mindbody-healing.com/positive-mental-attitude.html

## You Are Everything ~ Everything Is You

Become More of an Optimist [259]

Find Energy and Productivity with a Positive Attitude [260]

Quiz: Do You Have Positive Energy? [261]

Solve Your Problem: Gratitude Index [262]

Solve Your Problem: Positive Thinking Index [263]

The ABCs of Success [264]

The Benefits of Optimism [265]

The Optimism Quiz [266]

---

[259] http://stress.about.com/od/optimismspirituality/ht/optimisthowto.htm
[260] http://stress.about.com/od/optimismspirituality/a/positive_energy.htm
[261] http://altmedicine.about.com/library/weekly/bl_quiz_positive_energy.htm
[262] http://www.solveyourproblem.com/gratitude/index.shtml
[263] http://www.solveyourproblem.com/positive-thinking/index.shtml
[264] http://www.one-mind-one-energy.com/ABC-of-Success.html
[265] http://stress.about.com/od/optimismspirituality/a/optimismbenefit.htm
[266] http://stress.about.com/od/optimismspirituality/a/optimismquiz.htm

The Strangest Secret (Earl Nightingale) [267]

## Qigong

Miracles of Natural Healing [268]

Spring Forest Qigong [269]

## Stress Reduction

Living a Low-Stress Lifestyle [270]

Reduce Stress and Improve Your Life with Positive Self Talk [271]

## The Jesus Sutras

Another Look at Pelagius [272]

---

[267] http://www.thestrangestsecretmovie.com/
[268] http://www.chilel.com/
[269] http://www.springforestqigong.com/index.htm
[270] http://stress.about.com/c/ec/30.htm
[271] http://stress.about.com/od/optimismspirituality/a/positiveselftak.htm
[272] http://www.sullivan-county.com/z/pelagius2.htm

Church of the East [273]

Nestorian Steele [274]

Pelagianism Summary [275]

Pelagius [276]

Pelagius and Pelagianism [277]

The Nestorian Pages [278]

**Transcendental Consciousness**

Transcendental Consciousness [279]

Transcendental Consciousness [280]

---

[273] http://en.wikipedia.org/wiki/Church_of_the_East
[274] http://en.wikipedia.org/wiki/Nestorian_Stele
[275] http://www.bookrags.com/research/pelagianism-eorl-10/
[276] http://en.wikipedia.org/wiki/Pelagius
[277] http://members.tripod.com/british_muslims_assn/pelagius_and_pelagianism.html
[278] http://www.oxuscom.com/nestpage.htm
[279] http://www.transcendentalconsciousness.com/
[280] http://www.themystic.org/transcendental/index.htm

## Transcendental Meditation

Benefits of Transcendental Meditation [281]

Committee for Stress Free Schools [282]

David Lynch Foundation Videos [283]

Questions and Answers on the Transcendental Meditation Technique [284]

Transcendental Meditation Blog [285]

Transcendental Meditation Program [286]

## Transpersonal Consciousness

A Paradigm of Transpersonal Consciousness, Spirituality and Enlightenment [287]

---

[281] http://www.tm.org/benefits-of-meditation
[282] http://www.tmeducation.org/
[283] http://www.tmeducation.org/david-lynch-foundation-videos
[284] http://www.doctorsontm.com/questions-and-answers-on-tm
[285] http://www.tm.org/blog/
[286] http://www.tm.org/
[287] http://www.anunda.com/paradigm/index.htm

Permanent Peace [288]

Transpersonal Consciousness [289]

Triumph of the Spirit: Finding Peace and Purpose in a Chaotic World [290]

**Vedas**

Internet Sacred Text Archive: The Vedas [291]

The Vedas (Sacred Scriptures of Hinduism) [292]

Vedas [293]

Vedas and Upanishads [294]

---

[288] http://www.permanentpeace.org/overview/index.html
[289] http://www.paolaambrosi.com/transpercon.html
[290] http://bolstablog.wordpress.com/2009/12/06/braden-video/
[291] http://www.sacred-texts.com/hin/
[292] http://www.hinduwebsite.com/vedicsection/vedaindex.asp
[293] http://www.crystalinks.com/vedas.html
[294] http://www.san.beck.org/EC7-Vedas.html

## Vedic Knowledge

India Video Documentary Download (Deva Vision) [295]

Science of the Sacred [296]

Scientific Verification of Vedic Knowledge [297]

Scientific Verification of Vedic Knowledge (film) [298]

Vedic Knowledge [299]

## Vedic Science

Journal of Modern Science and Vedic Science [300]

Modern Science and Vedic Science [301]

---

[295] http://www.devavision.org/videos.html
[296] http://vedicsciences.net/sacred/science-of-sacred-2010.pdf
[297] http://www.archaeologyonline.net/artifacts/scientific-verif-vedas.html
[298] http://topdocumentaryfilms.com/scientific-verification-of-vedic-knowledge/
[299] http://www.vedicknowledge.com/what_is.html
[300] http://www.mum.edu/msvs/
[301] http://www.mum.edu/msvs/Chandler1.html

Vedic Science [302]

Vedic Science [303]

Vedic Science [304]

Vedic Science [305]

**Vision Boards**

How a Vision Board Works [306]

Vision Boards [307]

**Visualization**

How to Visualize and Use Affirmation Techniques [308]

---

[302] http://vedicsciences.net/
[303] http://maharishi-programmes.globalgoodnews.com/vedic-science/
[304] http://www.hindunet.org/vedicsciences/index.htm
[305] http://kevincarmody.com/vedic/vedic.html
[306] http://www.visionboardmanifesting.com/
[307] http://www.holistic-mindbody-healing.com/vision-boards.html
[308] http://www.holistic-mindbody-healing.com/how-to-visualize.html

Positive Visualization Exercises [309]

Solve Your Problem: Visualization Index [310]

The Healing Power of the Mind and Visualization [311]

The Power of Visualization and Affirmations [312]

**Voltaire Network**

The War on Libya, Part 1 [313]

The War on Libya, Part 2 [314]

The War on Libya, Part 3 [315]

---

[309] http://www.holistic-mindbody-healing.com/visualization-exercises.html
[310] http://www.solveyourproblem.com/visualization/index.shtml
[311] http://healing.about.com/od/visualization/a/powerofmind.htm
[312] http://www.holistic-mindbody-healing.com/power-of-visualization.html
[313] http://www.voltairenet.org/The-war-on-Libya-and-the-coming
[314] http://www.voltairenet.org/The-War-on-Libya-The-media
[315] http://www.voltairenet.org/The-War-on-Libya-The-Secret-NATO

## About the Author

Michele Doucette is webmistress of Portals of Spirit, a spirituality website whereby one will find links to (1) The Enlightened Scribe, (2) an ezine called Gateway To The Soul, (3) books of spiritual resonance as well as authors of metaphysical importance, (4) categories of interest from Angels to Zen, (5) up-to-date information as shared by a Quantum Healer, (6) affiliate programs and resources of personal significance, (7) healing resource advertisements and (8) spiritual news.

As a Level 2 Reiki Practitioner, she sends long distance Reiki to those who make the request, claiming only to be a facilitator of the Universal energy, meaning that it is up to the individual in question to use these energies in order to heal themselves.

Having also acquired a Crystal Healing Practitioner diploma (Stonebridge College in the UK), she is guardian to many from the mineral kingdom.

She is the author of several spiritual/metaphysical works; namely, *The Ultimate Enlightenment For 2012: All We Need Is Ourselves*, *Turn Off The TV: Turn On Your Mind*, *Veracity At Its Best*, *The Collective: Essays on Reality* (a composition of essays in relation to the Matrix), *Sleepers Awaken: The Time Is Now To Consciously Create Your Own Reality* and *Healing the Planet and Ourselves: How To Raise Your Vibration*, all of which have been published through St. Clair Publications. In addition, she has written a volume that deals with crystals, aptly entitled *The Wisdom of Crystals*.

She is also the author of *A Travel in Time to Grand Pré*, a visionary metaphysical novel that historically ties the descendants of Yeshua (Jesus) to modern day Nova Scotia. As shared by a reviewer, *Veracity At Its Best* "constructs the context for the spiritual message" imparted in *A Travel in Time to Grand Pré*.

Against the backdrop of 1754 Acadie, it was the blending of French Acadian history with current DNA testing that contributed to the weaving of this alchemical tale of time travel, romance and intrigue.

## You Are Everything ~ Everything Is You

From Henry I Sinclair to the Merovingians, from the Cathari treasure at Montségur to the Knights Templar, this novel, together with the words of Yeshua as spoken at the height of his ministry, has the potential to inspire others; for it is herein that we learn how individuals can find their way, their truth(s), so as to live their lives to the fullest.

www.ingramcontent.com/pod-product-compliance
Lightning Source LLC
Chambersburg PA
CBHW061642040426
42446CB00010B/1536